D1237457

Give Birth to Brightness

The Dial Press | *New York 1972*

Sherley Anne Williams

Give Birth to Brightness | A THEMATIC
STUDY IN NEO-BLACK LITERATURE

Library of Congress Cataloging in Publication Data

Williams, Sherley Anne, 1944–
  Give birth to brightness.

  Bibliography: p.
  1. American literature—Negro authors—History and
criticism. I. Title.
PS153.N5W54   810.9′8′96073   74–37446

Library of Congress Catalog Card Number: 74–37446

Printed in the United States of America
First Printing 1972

Designed by Jane Bvers Bierhorst

5

In another time and some other place, this book would have been dedicated to Professor Sterling Brown whose quiet questioning and prodding during interminable summer days forced me to clarify, expand and define, to pull together some sort of coherent whole out of a mass of half-thoughts; or to Nathan Heard who, out of the Blackness of his heart, brought the manuscript to the attention of a senior editor at Dial Press; or to Leah King who typed and retyped the manuscript, corrected spelling and any tendency toward swelled-headedness and depression—all at no extra charge. Without these people, this book would have been very difficult to create.

But, it is now, and each time I look into my son's eyes, I am reminded of the fragility of my own life, of the fact that in dying I would leave him nothing by which he would know me, through which he could see me define myself to myself in a public and vulnerable way. And because *Give Birth to Brightness* is, for me, a public statement of how I feel about and treasure one small aspect of Blackness in America,

THIS BOOK IS FOR MALCOLM

Contents

Note

Each part of this work is prefaced by quotations from poems selected from the works of Neo-Black writers. The quotations serve two functions. They indicate the thematic matter of each chapter and emphasize the commonality of themes and motifs which link the literary genres. For despite the fact that Neo-Black poetry receives only the barest mention in the present work, much of what is said about the novelists and the playwrights is also true of the poets. The use of poetry should also alert the reader to the fact that the material must be dealt with on at least two levels, the analytical and the emotional, for only through the use of both the objective and subjective vision can one hope to approach an understanding of what it means to be Black in America. This meaning in all its tender, terrifying and humorous beauty is what Black writers are interpreting and what Black critics must explicate.

Give Birth to Brightness

Introduction *A Thematic Study in Neo-Black Literature*

I wanted to know my mother when she sat
looking sad across the campus in the late 20's
into the future of the soul, there were black angels
straining above her head, carrying life from our ancestors,
and knowledge, and the strong nigger feeling. She sat
(in that photo in the yearbook I showed Vashti) getting into
new blues, from the old ones, the trips and passions
showered on her by her own. Hypnotizing me, from so far
ago, from that vantage of knowledge passed on to her passed on
to me and all the other black people of our time.
When I die, the consciousness I carry I will to
black people. May they pick me apart and take the
useful parts, the sweet meat of my feelings. And leave
the bitter bullshit rotten white parts
alone

Amiri Baraka
"leroy"
Black Magic: Poetry 1961–1967

In a poem published in 1965, Amiri Baraka (LeRoi Jones) proclaimed that "The Black Man is Making New Gods." To some extent, this summed up the many stutters and starts toward, if not "new gods," at least a new movement in Black literature which was then beginning to coalesce. Contemporary writers seemed more and more to be looking toward a Black universe whose landscape and personnel were Black. Thus, in 1962, Baraka said writers should be "erecting their own personal myths."[1] And later, K. William Kgositsile approached a criterion for contemporary Black literature in more nationalistic terms as he described writers who will be "destroying the symbols which have facilitated our captivity . . . creating and establishing symbols to facilitate our necessary constant beginning."[2] And finally in 1968, Hoyt Fuller posed the objective in more concrete terms, for the writers he speaks of are consciously and "deliberately striving to invest their work with the distinctive styles and rhythms and colors of the ghetto, with those peculiar qualities which, for example, characterize the music of a John Coltrane or a Charlie Parker or a Ray Charles."[3] Each of these statements has a common theme, that of talking about Black experiences in America from a Black perspective which cannot be limited or defined by those parochial frames of reference and value which are derived from and apply to traditions from which Black people have been largely excluded. The writers associated with this movement do not seek to be Black Hemingways or Ezra Pounds, Black Joyces or T. S. Eliots. They can never completely own the European and American traditions which fostered these writers. The European histories, conventions and traditions which inform the works of these writers with a continuing strength and vitality are the same ones which helped to ravage Africa, just as the American ones helped to enslave the children of Africa. For Black writers to seek expression totally within these traditions is to seek their own annihilation. Contemporary Black writers are turning their attention inward, seeking to identify the traditions of Black people, to explore their experiences, to define themselves and their people in images which grow out of their individual quests and group explorations. Rather than seeking entree into the mainstream of American writing—whether that mainstream be characterized by Bernard Malamud and John Updike or Leon Uris and Erich Segal—these writers have turned their attention to discovering and exploring, perhaps defining, the indigenous currents of Black experiences. Unlike many Black writers of previous generations, there is little feeling of writing as art for art's sake. Nor is the implicit audience for their work a faceless, but powerful, white society. On the contrary, these writers seem to be attempting to open a continuing conversation with Black people; their intended audience is Black.

The goal then, of the writers associated with the new

movement, is to communicate with, often to educate Black
people, to interpret their common and individual experiences, to reveal the beauty and pain, the ugliness and the
joy of four hundred years of living in the New World,
what this has done to Black people and, most importantly,
what it can and does mean to them. The interpretation
must, if it is to do this job without condescension and at
the same time preserve the uniqueness of this experience,
use symbols which have derived their meaning for Black
people out of that experience. Thus, instead of an expression of the "plight" of Black people as a means of edifying white people, Baraka and other writers seek to express
Black experiences as a means of edifying Blacks first and
whoever else can understand them second.[4]

A highly political, often violent literature has come
out of this movement in which poets and, to a lesser degree, playwrights, have emerged as spokesmen for what
appears to be small coteries of writers located in the large
urban centers of America. Many of these writers have
taken as their subject matter the many themes and stories
of the ghetto; ghetto English, the so-called Negro dialect,
is their language. The heroes of the ghetto streets become,
with modification, their heroes. Their avowed aim is "dehonkification," the liberating of the minds of Black people
from psychological slavery to the white man.[5]

The new movement has been variously described as the
Black aesthetics movement, Black consciousness, Black
arts, cultural nationalism and the cultural arm of the

Black revolution. In this work, the movement is called Neo-Black, "Neo" because the literature being created now often takes new and different forms in Black rituals, jazz poetics and fantastical visions in fiction, "Black" because, however light the skin coloring, it is the symbol of both the African and American origins of Black people. Neo-Black does not add just another term to the growing list of names which seek to define and describe this movement. Rather, it suggests continuity with the past and a reinterpretation of it instead of an abrupt break or sharp veering off into something entirely different from what has gone before. Black people have always been black; this, along with their distinctive features—the broad noses, thick lips and nappy hair—is what has set them apart from other Americans. This classic, stereotyped image of Black people is being reasserted. Now, however, the people whom it was meant to describe and limit are recovering and redefining the meanings of this image. Thus, Neo-Black literature does not proclaim, self-consciously, that the old Black, however one wants to define that, is dead, or gone, or that "it" was never more than a myth, a figment of someone's imagination. Rather, Black as person, history, tradition and culture is looked at with new eyes which attempt to discover and retrieve those things which may prove useful as Black people create a present which gives them dignity, positive self-images and economic strength.

A thematic examination of the Black literature which

has appeared during the last ten years shows that rather than being characteristic of a small coterie of writers, the avowed aims of Neo-Black writers unite a wide and diverse collection of writers who have never been vocal proponents of the Black aesthetics movement. For Neo-Black writing is neither cultist nor cabalistic, but rather a free-wheeling spirit which cuts across political and literary boundaries and genres and provides a common impetus for a disparate group of writers and critics, some of whom are among the most brilliant in the country.

This movement and the attitude toward Black life which characterizes it can be illustrated through an analysis of selected works by contemporary writers who represent varying degrees of public involvement with the movement in Black literature. The writers under discussion, Amiri Baraka, James Baldwin and Ernest Gaines, are individuals whose writings and public stances appear to have nothing in common except that all are Black and all write about Black people. In analyzing the works of these men, the object here is to examine and describe an aspect of Neo-Black literature rather than to define the literature itself. Neo-Black literature is still very much in the process of becoming and it is left to later writers and critics to set the criteria and pinpoint more precisely those characteristics which distinguish Neo-Black writing from that which has come before and that which will come after. Future generations of Black critics may even feel that the use of the term "Neo-Black" is premature, that what confronts the Black critic today is not a reaction against but a continuation of the line of Black fiction begun by Williams Wells Brown, the first published Black novelist, in 1853. This kind of long-range perspective is important to the present discussion, for the Black literature of the sixties and seventies developed out of this long line of Black fiction and is related to this literature by more than the use of the word "Black." Emphasis is placed on continuity, the continuous tradition of Black literature—both fiction and non-fiction, prose and poetry —for each of these aspects has been influenced by the others, and works are cited in varying and often complementary contexts so that one will always be aware of the many dimensions which each work embodies.

It is obvious that American Black literature is, by definition, a part of a larger whole. Black literature, and most particularly, Neo-Black literature, is a distinctive part of American literature with many similarities and sometimes identical characteristics. The thrust of this work, however, its major concern, is not with identifying parallel developments in white American history, culture and literature and Black American history, culture and literature, but with examining aspects of the Black literature as it portrays aspects of the Black experience in America. This does not, of course, rule out the possibility that similar developments have occurred in American or Western culture; it merely limits the degree to which they are examined in the present discussion.

INTRODUCTION

The surrealistic nightmare of Baraka's *Dutchman* and his version of racial warfare in *The Slave* provide the limits at one extreme for this study. At the other end is Baldwin's examination of the sexual basis of racism in *Blues for Mister Charlie* and the realistic, almost prosaic story of love and death in rural Louisiana in Gaines's *Of Love and Dust*. The central figures from Baraka's two plays, Clay in *Dutchman* and Walker in *The Slave*, are drawn from the Western literary tradition of the tormented central character whose doom is foreshadowed by the tragic flaw in his own nature. In Baraka's work, this tradition is tempered by the Black experience of America. By contrasting the two characters with Richard and Marcus, the central figures in *Blues for Mister Charlie* and *Of Love and Dust*, who are representative of heroic life styles drawn almost entirely from Black experience, one gains an insight into an emerging motif which may become a major theme in Neo-Black literature.

| II |

Baraka, in his poetry, is master of long, rhetorically complex phrases, tumbling one after another with an ever increasing momentum, capped by pithy expressions which sum up an attitude, a posture, a feeling in a few words. His politics are revolutionary and many of his poems and most of his plays are characterized by a lust for the white man's blood. Baraka's emergence as the leading exponent of Neo-Black writing is symbolic of the waning of that trend in Black literature in which writers addressed themselves to white audiences. This trend influenced not only the great autobiographies of Frederick Douglass (*Life and Times*, 1892), Richard Wright (*Black Boy*, 1945), and Malcolm X (*The Autobiography of Malcolm X*, 1964), but the essays of W. E. B. DuBois (*Souls of Black Folk*, 1903) and James Baldwin (*Notes of a Native Son*, 1956; *Nobody Knows My Name*, 1961; and *The Fire Next Time*, 1964) and the novels of Wright (*Native Son*, 1940), Ralph Ellison (*Invisible Man*, 1952), and Anne Petry (*The Street*, 1946), among others, as well as the early plays of Amiri Baraka (*Dutchman* and *The Slave*, 1964). Some of the best literary works by Blacks are included in this list; all of those cited are characterized by their assumption that their audience is white and in them, as Cecil Brown observes, "the scene is America, the time is Now and the characters are forever me and you and Charles."[6]

Neo-Black literature, however, is distinguished from older literary works by the fact that it is a literature centered around a continuing conversation among Black people. One can see the change in Baraka's works, particularly in the volume of poetry *Black Magic: Poetry 1961–1967* and in the plays *Black Mass* and *Madheart*. The characters change from "me and you and Charles" to me and you and the Black man (or woman), or on another level, the emphasis shifts from the racial conflict as a theme to the problem of how a Black man gets himself together, which may—and often does—involve racial confrontations.

Dutchman and *The Slave* were first produced in the middle of that turbulent decade of the sixties. The civil rights demonstrations of the early sixties were begun in non-violence yet often led to violence against the demonstrators. Stokely Carmichael's cry for Black power seemed to cleave the decade, as well as the civil rights movement, in half. And the bloody urban riots of the later sixties made the Watts rebellion of 1965 look like a picnic. The tension which characterized the decade also informs these plays. Yet, in analyzing the plays, one finds that one also analyzes their limitations as vehicles for Black expression. Their scenes and dialogues speak more to that aspect of Black life in which one tries to adjust to or gain some understanding from white society—without first being sure that one has adjusted to or understood one's self as part of and in relation to all Black people. *Dutchman* and *The Slave* thus serve as a point of reference so that one can begin to understand the necessity and urgency of the themes posited by the writings of Neo-Black artists.

James Baldwin has long been accorded the status of spokesman for and about Black people. And if he no longer occupies that position, it is perhaps to his advantage. Critics of Baldwin's literary works have usually dealt more with those statements uttered in his role as

spokesman or with his alleged homosexuality than with
his plays, novels or short stories. Eldridge Cleaver, for
example, questions the masculinity of the central character, Rufus, in *Another Country*—and Baldwin's own
masculinity—but skirts the problem of what Baldwin is
trying to say about the Black man as artist, lover and
human being. Rufus Scott, the Black protagonist, in becoming involved with a Southern white woman, returns
not to the traditional source of his people's strength, but
to the centuries-old source of their agony. The subsequent
sexual relationship, based as it is on unresolved love-hate
feelings, paralyzes him so that he is unable to relate his
personal experience to the patterns of culture and tradition which could have been a sustaining source of strength
for him. Thus, unable either to give or receive love, he
jumps off a bridge in New York. Cleaver sees in Rufus
merely "a pathetic wretch who indulged in the white
man's pastime of committing suicide,"[7] and by his recita-
tion of Rufus' "flaws"—his homosexual connection with
one of the white characters in the book, his relationship
with a Southern white woman—he seeks to prove that the
character, Rufus, is less masculine than Richard Wright's
literary creation, Bigger Thomas (*Native Son,* 1940),
just as he seeks to prove that Baldwin is less masculine
than Wright. Cleaver is on the trail of what he calls the
"ghost," the homosexual in Baldwin, a hunt which does
not permit him to deal with the serious Black theme of
tradition as a living and necessary support in the lives

of Black people, a theme which is a major force in the
novel. This is typical of the kind of reaction Baldwin
evokes from critics, for his personal life rather than his
art is usually the subject of the criticism.[8] Critics have
generally failed to see that heritage and culture as a sustaining force in the lives of Black people is a recurring
theme in Baldwin's writings, first stated in the short story,
"Sonny's Blues" (1957), and one which he returns to in
Blues for Mister Charlie.

The outlines of the theme are the basis for this early
short story. In *Another Country* Baldwin again approaches the theme, this time from the perspective of a
central character who is haunted and finally overcome by
the castration impulse of American society. In *Blues,*
Baldwin comes full circle, restating the theme against the
backdrop of the faltering civil rights movement. The play,
the novel and the short story are a triptych which captures
and gives an increasingly larger insight into one form of
Black interactions with history, culture and life. Baldwin
has no public links with the younger, often more militant
writers, but in this theme his concerns are similar to theirs.

Ernest Gaines appears, by contrast with Baraka and
Baldwin, almost apolitical, for his public life is contained
in his published novels and short stories and the brief
biographical statements which appear on the back pages
of his books. He uses little of the flashy brilliance which
the characters of Baldwin and Baraka often employ to
describe and analyze history, society and themselves. Yet

his technique, while different, is just as good. The un-
forced ease and power with which his stories unfold is
proof of that. His stories derive that power and ease from
an approximation of the rhythm of Black speech and,
through it, Black lives. Jane Pittman, the one hundred
twenty-year-old ex-slave who is the central character in
his recent novel, *The Autobiography of Miss Jane Pittman*, speaks in a rambling yet evocative Black speech.
Her images and metaphors are largely those of rural
Louisiana, the only place she has ever known. She symbolizes the constancy of the past, the will toward self-
definition and control of destiny which has always
informed Black experiences in America. Miss Jane is the
past and the present, the struggle toward the future. The
wiry spirit which is liberated in the changing of her name,
from Ticey to Jane, during the Civil War and forcibly
caged during the repressions of Reconstruction and its
bloody aftermath at last finds expression in defiance of the
plantation owner when Miss Jane continues on a freedom
march against his wishes. This concluding act of personal
defiance repeats the act of defiance which begins the novel
when Miss Jane refuses to respond to her mistress who has
called her by the slave name. The past, here, is a living
force which struggles to make the spirit of past events
manifest in the still oppressive present.

Gaines, like Baldwin and Baraka, is also concerned
with Black life as it is informed and affected by the traditions and patterns of the past. This is a clearly defined

element in his novel, *Of Love and Dust*; here, however, the hero breaks away from the confines of tradition and in doing so infuses new life and, perhaps, a new direction into a past which restrains more than it liberates or supports. The novel, *Of Love and Dust*, and the play, *Blues for Mister Charlie*, are variations on a common theme, the interplay between the individual and the group, the outsider and the tradition, the streetman and the collective Black experience. This theme also provides a common point of departure for other writers and unites them under the rubric, Neo-Black.

By focusing then, on selected works by these writers and the male characters who dominate the works, one can see that however divided they are by politics or public stances, the writers have a vision of Black life in common. For these main characters are representative of a life style which has come to seem particularly Black, the life of the "cool," the "hip," the "street." The emergence as heroic figures of characters drawn from this life style is indicative of a growing desire among Black writers to explore Black existence and life from the inside as life experiences which have significance in and of themselves rather than as a culturally deprived heritage which takes its significance and meaning from the fact that it has been a source of irritation and embarrassment for white America. One can call these literary characters, "the worst type of Negro," as does Edward Margolies,[9] but to do so overlooks some essential facts about the connotational values of the word hero—and anti-hero—and more importantly some essential facts about the Black experience in America.

Notes: Introduction

1. LeRoi Jones, "The Myth of a Negro Literature," an address given at the American Society for African Culture, March 14, 1962, *Home: Social Essays* (New York: Morrow & Co., 1966), p. 112.

2. K. William Kgositsile, "Towards Our Theatre: A Definitive Act," *Negro Digest* (April 1967), p. 16.

3. Hoyt Fuller, "Towards a Black Aesthetics," in *Black Expression*, Addison Gayle, Jr., ed. (New York: Weybright & Tally, Inc., 1969), p. 269.

4. Mari Evans, "Contemporary Black Literature," *Black World* (June 1970), p. 93.

5. The Black psychiatrist, Dr. Price Cobb, is credited with coining "dehonkification"; the sentiment can be found in the writings of most of the vocal Neo-Black writers. Amiri Baraka, Ed Bullins, Don L. Lee, Marvin X and Nikki Giovanni have all expressed this idea in one way or another.

6. Cecil Brown, "Black Literature and LeRoi Jones," *Black World* (June 1970), p. 29.

7. Eldridge Cleaver, "Notes on a Native Son," *Soul on Ice* (New York: Dell Pub. Co., 1968), p. 107.

8. Baldwin's personality has engaged the attention of critics to such an extent that Addison Gayle, Jr. felt it necessary to write "A Defence of James Baldwin," *College Language Association Journal (CLA)* X (March 1966), 201–208.

9. Edward Margolies, *Native Sons* (Philadelphia: J. B. Lippincott, 1968), p. 125.

I Regenesis

| I |

Growth can sit there from
a far corner
staring its years into your
brow: of thoroughfares run undulating
across the pride of nature's ebony likeness

| II |

A generation in chaos
an old legion in fear
a country in terror of its shame
the sleep of past progressions endowed
in the bowels of this land

. . . .

| III |

Growth sits on a pane
of glass
looking out at the seed
of decay it has shed
from itself: from
within, the seed rocks furiously
to the frenzy of a people
caught in revolution.

Ron Welburn
from "Regenesis"
The New Black Poetry

CHAPTER ONE

The Heroic Tradition in Black America

She's blacker
than the night which holds
us in communion
against the white picket fences.
There's clash in her eyes,
and she smiles whitely
to the tambourines.
There's a folk song audience
of rebels who lover
her mother into children,
and then the children,
and they're all in the roads
searching for the art
which makes singing
a blessing of hatred.

Michael Harper
"Blues Alabama"
Dear John, Dear Coltrane

| I |

Despite the fact that this is not an historical study of Black literature, the historical perspective must be considered. If one believes with Arna Bontemps that time is a pendulum and not a river,[1] the swing of the literary pendulum begun during the so-called Harlem Renaissance is ap-

33

parently being repeated in the efforts of Neo-Black writers to create new images of Blackness and to explore relatively untouched areas of Black experiences. Certainly, many of the critical statements of that era have a contemporary tone, as, for example, Alain Locke's statements in "The New Negro," the essay which became the philosophical manifesto of the Renaissance.

. . . for generations in the mind of America, the Negro has been more of a formula than a human being—a something to be argued about, condemned or defended, to "be kept down," or "in his place," or "helped up," be worried with or worried over, harassed or patronized, a social bogey or social burden. The thinking Negro even has been induced to share this same general attitude, to focus his attention on controversial issues, to see himself in the distorted perspective of a social problem. His shadow, so to speak, has been more real to him than his personality.[2]

Yet, their very contemporaneousness indicates that the problems outlined in them have yet to be resolved, the solutions are still to be achieved. The fact that Alain Locke's statements are still being echoed in the militant documents of the present has its roots in complex sociopolitical factors. Some portion of it also lies in the nature of the developing literary tradition which Locke's statements were meant to protest against. The main current in Black literature had always been political; Black literature had been created to serve various social and/or political aims in a forthright and, at times, unadorned manner. It was an expression of a limited aspect of the lives of Black people and led readers "to believe that in Negro life there exists no tradition, no field of manners, no possibility of ritual intercourse such as may, for example, sustain the Jew even after he has left his father's house."[3]

Slave poets, such as Phillis Wheatley, were educated as an experiment to prove that Blacks were educable and could be literary in the same way in which whites were literary.[4] Phillis Wheatley's poetry is representative of the Neo-Classic verse of her time; certainly, it is no worse than the general level of colonial American verse and, at times, it is much better. Her concern as a poet was not to present the uniqueness of slave experiences in colonial New England, but to reflect the orthodox European views of Christianity and, when she touched upon it at all, African savagery. Other early Black poets wrote to prove they could, and at least one, George Moses Horton, wrote to gain his freedom.[5] Their poems rarely reflected the culture or lives of Black people whether free or enslaved. At its best, the poetry is a muted, artificial counterpoint; to the polemical, often strident, prose and fiction which grew out of the anti-slavery campaigns of the mid-nineteenth century.

The most vital, indeed, the dominant tradition of Black literature is rooted in the essays and the narratives of escaped and freed slaves. The narratives, which Sterling Brown calls "literary weapons,"[6] are accounts of oppression and wrongs, "a history," as Charles Nichols states, "of the struggle to establish human rights in America."[7] The narratives provide a limited access into the private and personal worlds of the slaves. One sees some of the devices and pretenses which enabled Black people to survive the horrifying experience of slavery, and the rebellious attitudes which often existed behind servile masks. Yet, it is also clear from these narratives that whatever descriptions of Black traditions or "field of manners" are given are there either to point up the effects of slavery, or are unintentional by-products. The major impetus of these men as writers was the need to call attention to the plight of Black people in this country, to point out the inequities and horrors of America's caste system, to provide answers and solutions to the American dilemma. The literary descendents of the prose writers, the early novelists, were prompted by much the same needs and desires.

Sterling Brown, in *The Negro in American Fiction*, calls many of these novelists "counter-propagandists" and dates the beginning of this movement from the publication of Sutton Griggs's *Unfettered* in 1902.[8] But the movement begins with William Wells Brown's *Clotel or the President's Daughter* in 1853. These propaganda novels have in common a kind of hybrid tradition developed through a welding of the melodramatic aspects of European Romantic traditions and the problems and concerns of Black people in America. The primary qualities of melodrama are thrilling action, numerous coincidences and improbable or unusual situations in which good,

represented by the hero, and evil, represented by the villain, battle for dominance in the world. The improbable
devices created to balk the hero are important only in so
far as he, by equally improbable means, triumphs over
them and is united (or reunited) with the heroine in a life
that is lived happily ever after.[9] Using this structure as a
medium for urging the right of Black people to a better
place in society, novelists such as Griggs, Charles Chesnutt and W.E.B. Du Bois continued to objectify the classic
battle between the forces of virtue and evil in the society.
The Black hero was the embodiment of virtue and fought
to make this virtue known to those forces—the unrecon-
structed white man who was the villain—which tried to
keep this virtue hidden. The wedding between melodramatic structure and racial themes was logical. The stuff
of the average Black person's life, when seen from the
perspective of white America, was unusual, even improbable, dangerous and exciting. The melodramatic form
highlights these very characteristics. This fusion produced
the novels of Griggs and Chesnutt and a score of others,
whose significance is more historical than literary; but it
also produced James Weldon Johnson's interesting novel,
The Autobiography of an Ex-Colored Man, and many of
the best pieces of contemporary Black literature.

If one is to take Langston Hughes's comment in *The
Nation* at face value, exploring Black tradition was not a
high priority for the young rebellious Black writers of the
twenties. His statement that "We younger Negro writers

. . . intend to express our individual dark-skinned selves without fear or shame" has often been quoted. The remarks which follow this rather revolutionary statement— always before the idea had been to prove that Black writers, except for the accident of skin color, were much like white writers—are just as revealing though seldom quoted: "If white people are pleased, we are glad. If they are not, it doesn't matter. We know we are beautiful. And ugly too. The tom tom cries and the tom tom laughs. If colored people are pleased, we are glad. If they are not, their displeasure doesn't matter either."[10] Hughes comes very close to a restatement of the late nineteenth century concept of art for art's sake. There is also, however, an attempt on the part of these younger writers to see themselves as much as possible through their own eyes, to rid themselves of the confining political themes and parochial gentility which had been the overriding characteristics of Black expression since the middle of the nineteenth century. Perhaps the swing from the overt social consciousness of the early writers to the opposite extreme of abandoning the politically persuasive aspect of literature was necessary in order for these writers to get a perspective on themselves as Blacks and as artists. This seems to be the deeper meaning in Locke's statement:

Through having to appeal from the unjust stereotypes of the [the Blackman's] oppressors and traducers to those of his liberators, friends and benefactors he has had to subscribe to the traditional positions from which his case has been viewed. Little true social or self-understanding could come from such a situation.[11]

These traditional positions had to be attacked, torn down, gotten beyond before the writers could have an unobscured view of themselves. It is this attempt which provides the impetus for the Black writings of the twenties.

The most characteristic Black expression of the Renaissance, the inverted symbolism which posited new referents for the verbal symbols of "primitive" and "civilized," was an effort to get beyond these "traditional positions." In the works of Black writers, what had been considered ignorant, crude, even animalistic in the European value system as it applied to Black people became an age-old wisdom, a straightforward honesty and an irrepressible capacity to enjoy life. The characters in these works were often drawn from and depicted against the lowest economic and social strata of Harlem—which was seen as a microcosm of Black communities, a Black nation within a larger white one. Middle-class Blacks, the "strivers" and "dicties," who outwardly, at least, showed an adherence to the values and mores of white society, were held up to scorn. A highly romanticized Africanesque atmosphere pervades the literature. This is not the Africa of animalistic brutality so often seen in the works of white writers but one of splendor and an almost Adamic freedom. Africa is evoked not only through concrete symbols, but through the evocation of what Alain Locke called "tropical nonchalance," and Rudolph Fisher "the characteristic grin" of the Black man, his acceptance of situations, "not with resignation but with amusement."[12]

The classic use of inverted symbolism in fiction is the

work of Claude McKay. *Home to Harlem*, in its either/or
structure—either one must be the vigorous, natural Black
man who has remained relatively untouched by a sterile,
spirit-destroying Western civilization or be the misfit
Black intellectual alienated from both the white and Black
worlds—is representative of the problems which confronted the writers who attempted to work with these symbols in fiction. The story is the loosely structured episodic
adventures of Jake, a semi-skilled roving laborer, a vet-
eran of the Great War, as he looks for the beautiful prostitute, Felice, whom he met on his first night home in
America. He moves through the jazz life of Harlem, the
clubs and cabarets and parties, meeting the entertainers,
the prostitutes, pimps, bootleggers and sweet men—
"kept" men—who frequent the world and, finally, feeling
the need to get away from Harlem for a while, he takes a
job as fourth cook on a train. There he comes into contact
with Ray, an educated Haitian who is a waiter on the train.
The lives of the two men never really meet, despite their
close association. Jake is the "natural" man, man in the
carefree, happy yet socially responsible state as yet unfettered by the restraints and neuroses of modern civilization.
Ray is the "civilized" Black man whose education, while
still allowing him to value and appreciate the life style
which Jake epitomizes, has also made him forever the
lonely observer rather than a joyous participant in that
life. The conflict which McKay seeks to establish never ma-
terializes. Jake and Ray are presented more as opposite
sides of one nature; Jake the elemental emotional half,

Ray the thinking articulate half. But they are not in conflict with each other. Rather, they are both in revolt against the restraints of society. Because Jake's revolt is unconscious, instinctual, he is never pulled in conflicting directions. There is no discrepancy between the life he wants and the life he leads. Ray's rebellion never passes the intellectual stage; he never does more than verbalize his sense of estrangement and discontent. McKay sets up a contrast, rather than a conflict, which tells little more than the differences between the two characters. The novel fails technically, for even in this contrast Ray often appears as little more than an artificial contrivance for McKay to convey the themes which he has been unable to depict through narration or characterization. McKay also has problems with the jazz life as a symbol of a more unrestrained environment. Jake, the natural man, is often disgusted by what he sees around him. There was, McKay tells the reader, "something . . . naturally beautiful about his presence," which made him stand out from others. He has what he himself calls spirit, "a strange elusive something" which he senses in the prostitute, Felice. He moves through Harlem and other eastern cities, a part of and participant in the jazz life but also removed from it in a way which is at odds with what McKay seems to be trying to convey: the superiority of the vigorous Black demi-world over the sterility of white America. It is only when McKay internalizes the civilized-primitive conflict within one character and against more clearly defined cultural differences as he does in Bita in *Banana Bottom* (1931) that he begins to make the kind of telling statements about the failures of Western civilization of which he was capable.

The ill-defined correspondence between symbol and referent invites Benjamin Brawley's comment that: "[the younger writers] protest against the older stereotypes; yet if they do not watch, they will give us new stereotypes hardly better than the old."[13] It is not, however, a question of evaluating the new stereotypes on their worth as accurate or valid representations of Black people or even the part which these stereotypes may have played in, as one Black reviewer charged, pleasing white readers as "pure coon-stuff" which is important.[14] Rather, it is the fact that Renaissance writers were beginning to question whether being different, in some ways, from whites was an automatic sign of inferiority. They attempted to confront what has become a traditional problem for the Black artist: How to depict and express the culture of Black people, the ritualized patterns and traditions which have enabled Black people to survive the terrifying experience of being made American. The only art form which has consistently drawn in an identifiable and valid manner upon Black life in America, which reflects that life, is music. Part of the difficulty of the Black artist lies in the fact that, most often, it has been white scholars who "discovered" and "defined" what is Black, what is a fusion of the bits and pieces of an African past and an ever-changing American present. An artist needs to use his personal and group experiences, his culture and himself, as a touchstone for his art, and the Black artist in America has had to discover methods of creating a distinctive Black art even though the question, What is Black? has been answered for the most part by white people. Black music provides its own answers to the questions in the raucous sounds of Ray Charles, in the haunting lyric solos of John Coltrane, in the piety and jubilance of Mahalia Jackson's gospels. And the process is unconscious, non-verbal. But a writer deals in awareness and he creates verbal statements out of his experience.

The Black writers of the Renaissance and most of the writers who came after them tended to verbalize their experiences by seeking to refute or confirm the racial stereotypes which governed their lives, drawing upon their backgrounds to do this but seldom bringing to their writing fresh or original modes of expression from their roots. Their literature was, thus, almost always reactionary because these writers were responding to symbols already created to embody what was to them a partially alien tradition. The symbols themselves represented the forces which oppressed the writers.

Jean Toomer's experimental novel, *Cane* (1923), differs from *Home to Harlem* not only in technical proficiency but in Toomer's apparent realization that it was not always necessary to look outside the limits of Black experience for symbols and images with which he could embody his themes. In this, he is more akin to contemporary writers, a precursor in method of the Black writers who seemed to have jumped with startling suddenness onto the literary scene, the Neo-Black writers. The book is made up of poems, sketches, stories and a novella in quasi-dramatic form. The first part of the book is set in the South, the stories and poems of the second part are set in the North. In the novella, "Kabnis," the setting is once more the South, a symbolic and rhetorical return to the beginning, to Black roots in America. Toomer draws a line between the North and the South, the Black and the near white. The book's loose thematic unity is centered around the South as the spiritual homeland of Blacks. Toomer juxtaposes the vital and often violent nature and circumstances of rural Southern Blacks with the enervated lives of urban, middle-class Blacks. The South is viewed as both womb and crucible, for it gives birth to strong hardy natives and helps those who return to and accept it to forge a strength to withstand the harshness of their daily lives. "Song of the Son," the beautifully evocative poem from the first part of the book, finds an echo to its lines:

O land and soil, red soil and sweet gum tree,
. . . .

Thy son, in time, I have returned to thee,
Thy son, I have in time returned to thee.
. . . .

O Negro slaves, dark purple ripened plums,
Squeezed, and bursting in the pine-wood air,
Passing, before they stripped the old tree bare
One plum was saved for me, one plum becomes

An everlasting song, a singing tree,
Caroling softly souls of slavery,

What they were, and what they are to me,
Caroling softly souls of slavery.[15]

in Kabnis' thought: "If I could feel that I came to the
South to face [the South]. If I, the dream (not what is
weak and afraid in me) could become the face of the
South." And again, one of the characters in the novella
sees in Kabnis "a vision . . . a promise of soil-soaked
beauty; uprooted, thinning out. Suspended a few feet
above the soil whose touch would resurrect him." What is
weak and afraid in Kabnis wins out; he does not find the
spiritual regeneration he seeks in his homeland. But the
pessimism of Kabnis' decline is balanced and overshad-
owed by the strength of spirit shown by Carrie Sue and
Lewis who accept and internalize the challenge of the
South. The theme of the South as regenerative place also
finds expression in the work of W.E.B. Du Bois, particularly in the collection of essays, *The Souls of Black Folk*,
and in James Weldon Johnson's *Autobiography of An Ex-
Colored Man*. Toomer does not see the lives of the folk,
poverty stricken rural Blacks, as mere manifestations of
exotic life styles, nor does he depict their ways in direct
contrast to a decadent Western civilization. Rather, the
violence which informs so much of their lives becomes
synonymous with life and the will to live. The life of the
body and that of the spirit must be sustained through
violent confrontations, usually with whites. A retreat from
those confrontations thus becomes a retreat from life. The
implication is that the would-be whites, those who because
of skin color or conscious choice seek to disassociate them-

selves from lower-class Blacks, have made this kind of retreat. A deadly ennui uninformed by any sense of vitality is the result. There is an opaque, almost cryptic beauty in the stories and poems and the play; their quiet pacing is at odds with the often violent, tumultuous events they depict. Even as Toomer attempts to reveal the larger significance of these events in the present, he implies that acceptance of a painful, often humiliating past is a necessary adjunct for the spiritual liberation of Blacks.

Toomer succeeds in illuminating the larger philosophical implications which are inherent in the daily lives of ordinary Black people and in this sense he moves toward the necessary revelation of a Black mythology which speaks to Black people in their individual as well as their collective identities, in their actual as well as their symbolic representations.

While not usually discussed in connection with the Renaissance, Ralph Ellison's *Invisible Man* must be considered in the present context. Ellison begins, in this novel, to plant on some of the fertile ground first turned by Renaissance writers. His use of Black music as symbol and rhetorical device, his use of folklore and folk character are all within the realm of convention utilized so extensively in the works of Sterling Brown, Langston Hughes, Jean Toomer, Rudolph Fisher and Claude McKay. As in the best works by these authors, Ellison's use of Black styles never degenerates to the level of mere exoticism or decoration. And, unlike most of his immediate contemporaries, Ellison used the Black experience as a commentary upon the plight of humanity—rather than using the plight of the Black man as an end in itself. He fuses symbols from Black life with symbols from Western literary tradition to create a symbolic language which is uniquely personal, yet uniquely universal.

The novel details the episodic adventures of a young Black man as he moves from his small Southern home town to a small Southern Black college, through an urban industrial work experience in a paint factory in the North, a partially regenerative sojourn in the home of Mary Rambo, an earthy woman who, as a symbolic mother, is the connecting link between the Southern and Northern experiences, and a frustrating involvement with a white organization, the Brotherhood. This last adventure culminates in a riot in Harlem and the protagonist goes into hibernation in a basement room. He finally realizes that through all his adventures he has been invisible, that what people responded to was not him but what they wanted him to be. On one very obvious level, the novel depicts the collective maturation experience of Black men; on another, it symbolizes the journey of Black people from slavery to the middle of the twentieth century. Each episode is significant on one or more levels, but those things which emerge as symbols are especially important.

The Battle Royal, fought by Black youths for the amusement of a group of white businessmen, and Men's House, home of status seeking Black males who go to jobs as janitors and porters dressed in expensive business suits, are symbols of the physical and mental subjugation of Blacks and the conquest of Black masculinity through the use of situations which render the very maleness of the Blacks ridiculous and therefore impotent. Chitterlings, the discarded table scraps of the whites, and sweet potatoes, both of which symbolize slavery and subjugation, become a ritual feast for those who accept themselves and their American history; sunglasses, which the hero uses as part of a conscious pose when his naïveté leads him into physical danger, symbolize the fronts through which Black men view a hostile world, laugh at it and attempt to manipulate it, all the while retaining a measure of anonymity and safety; these combine with more conventional symbols to form an Ellisonesque landscape against which he discusses identity, selfhood, subjugation and freedom.

The novel itself might almost be characterized as a journey from certainty to uncertainty, and the protagonist's very ambivalence about the meaning of his experiences, an ambivalence which is his one mainstay at the end of the novel, points toward a direct existence in his own mind. The protagonist is sure that whatever the significance of his own personal trip, he is not the American's Negro, whether that American be capitalist or communist, white liberal or Black something else. He sees the necessity of redefining himself in his own terms, terms which, while rooted in his history and traditions, take account of his present and future possibilities. And, in redefining himself in his own terms, he must create a new language to describe his new point of reference.

| II |

Neo-Black writers in America seem to be giving form and structure to what may appear to be formless and even chaotic Black experiences, creating from materials and experiences already available, following in the wake of whatever revolution or change in attitudes is taking place, rather than leading. This is probably true of all writers, but the American Black man as his own mythologist must of necessity recount his myth in the language of his historic oppressor. However, as Janheinz Jahn says:

The slave captures in his own and the slave master's language, a culture the master did not create and cannot control, which he, the slave, has recognized as his own. But in the process the language is transformed, acquiring different meanings which the master never expected. The slave becomes "bilingual." That language he shares with the master and the language he has minted from it are no longer identical. The slave breaks out of the prison of the master's language. This provides a new point of departure.[16]

One can see Jahn's theory of redefinition or reinterpretation in the changes which Black people have wrought in the meaning of the word "black." One finds that the dictionary defines the word "black" as gloomy, dismal, soiled, stained, angry, threatening, evil, malignant, wicked, etc., etc., and, when used as a noun, as a member of the Negro race.[17] Negroes are thus, by definition, evil, malignant, soiled, theatening, etc., etc. Yet Black people, in the process of acquiring a more positive group identity, have redefined the word so that Black is now beautiful and stands not only for positive images—truth, humaneness, strength, manliness and femininity—but for the socio-political revolutionary or radical who will not accept compromise on questions of equality or progress for Afro-Americans and for the lover of all people of African descent. Now whether or not one can find these last definitions or connotations in the dictionary or whether they are accepted by whites is of little concern and is not at all the point. The real point is this: An increasingly large body of Afro-Americans accept these definitions and even more understand them.[18]

This same kind of process has been instrumental in redefining the word "negro." However, here redefiniton has gone in the opposite direction, from the struggle during the early part of the twentieth century to have the word capitalized and thus imply respect for Afro-Americans as a race, to the Muslim's "so-called Negro," implying that "negro" is the white man's name for people of African descent and, therefore, can be nothing but a derogatory label, to the present-day usage where, in more radical or militant circles, "negro" takes its place on a revolutionary or radical spectrum somewhere between Black, which is beautiful and good, and colored, which is white and weak. The closest standard American English synonym to negro would probably be compromiser or appeaser—as opposed to outright traitor. Here again, an increasingly large number of Black people, while perhaps not using the terms in these new connotative senses, are aware that the connotations can be evoked.

A similar kind of transformation or metamorphosis has given birth to much of the vocabulary for Afro-American English, the so-called negro dialect. Even Anglo-Saxon curse words take on a new dimension when used by Black Americans. Witness the spate of cases in which Blacks, accused of insulting policemen or other officials by using what these officials have termed profane and lewd language, cite as part of their defense, the fact that these words have a different and often commendatory meaning in the vocabulary of ghetto Blacks. In at least one case in California, this defense has been successful.[19]

No one can say for certain how the new and different connotations of these and other words have evolved. In the case of the word Black, however, it is safe to say that its "choice" as the symbol of a new and positive feeling of selfhood on the part of Afro-Americans was not a random one. In using the word Black, Afro-Americans affirmed the very fact which had been so long denied or at least by-sided with the use of neutral terms such as brown, colored, negro: the fact of Blackness. The redefinition is couched in terms which have meaningful and positive values for Afro-Americans. Through this process, the American conflict is again drawn in its original terms, Black and white. And, most importantly, the oppressor's word has become the property of the oppressed.

Neo-Black writers have thus gone beyond the use of the
Black dialect to establish verisimilitude; nor is Black
speech in their writings used to caricature, to denote
uneducated, often unintelligent characters whose primary
function in the plot is comic relief. Rather, Black speech
becomes in their works—as it had in the works of Hughes
and Brown before them—a serious literary language
whose cadences and rhythms evoke a frame of reference
and value which is different from that which can be portrayed through the use of the standard dialect. This distinctive Black frame of reference is often the context out
of which one must define the words which are common to
both Black and white speech in America. The word
"hero" and its connotational values are very much to the
point.

The word "hero" has gone through almost as many
definition changes as the word "black" so that now one
finds it defined in the *Dictionary of Literary Definitions*
as no more than the central male character in a book or
play.[20] If that is all the word means, then it follows that
the term "anti-hero" has no significance and its definition
no literary meaning. While the literary definition of
"hero" or "heroic" may have changed, it is obvious that a
certain connotative value remains and it is this connotative value which is placed in opposition and gives meaning to the "anti" in the term "anti-hero."

Anti-hero as a descriptive term covers a wide variety of
character types stretching all the way from the hustler or

hipster to the freak, the outsider and the scapegoat.[21] The basic characteristic which is common to all and which links them in a kind of impotent rebellion against society is their quarrel with the culture from which they come. This quarrel has been the particular concern of the literature of the last two centuries—where the self is in a standing quarrel with its culture.[22]

Yet, anti-hero is not merely another word for hero. The term itself calls into question concepts which have played a large and important role for centuries prior to the emergence of a character type which stands in opposition to all the values which hero connotes. The hero as a symbol of certain values—which shifted as the values of the society shifted—has always been a rather fragmented concept. That is, there have always been many types of characters which fitted under this heading. The hero as warrior, lord or knight is the aristocratic hero who most often served as the heroic model for literary epics and romances. He might be either tragic or comic, depending upon whether his nature, in one respect or another, was badly flawed. If it was, his goals were frustrated and he came to an unhappy end. The comic hero was not comic because of his humorous personality, necessarily, but because he achieved his goals and the problem of the play or book or poem was resolved in his favor. All of these heroes have in common the fact that whatever their heroic posture, whatever values they were meant to symbolize or embody, their stance was one of support rather than questioning or quarreling with or rebelling against the values of the society in which they lived. The villain as a main character might be considered heroic; even here, however, his ultimate defeat, as in Shakespeare's *Richard III*, symbolizes the triumph of society over those forces which would destroy it.

The folk heroes, the heroes of the lower classes, who championed the rights of the poor against the rich approach the anti-heroic. The legends about Robin Hood, the best known of the English folk heroes, can be interpreted as the outlaw's attempt to have the economic and political system of fourteenth century England administered fairly; or as a revolt against all of the trappings of civilization, for Robin rejects his rightful place as heir to the Earl of Huntingdon and returns to the life of freedom and adventure with his men in Sherwood forest. The former definition is a kind of heroic posture in the aristocratic or classical sense, for it questions not the basic structure of society but merely asks that that structure be administered according to the rules already laid down. The latter interpretation is anti-heroic, for as Ihab Hassan notes of the hero/anti-hero question:

The gradual process of atrophy of the hero may have begun with Don Quixote, or perhaps even Job, or Orestes, and Christ. It enters the critical phase, however, only late in the eighteenth century. Goethe's Werther introduces the "tragic" Romantic hero who, in his inordinate conception of himself, severs the traditional bond between the hero and his society, and points the way to such extreme stances of alienation as were to find expression in the Byronic and Sadist hero, in the gothic and demonic protagonist, in werewolf, ghoul, and vampire. . . . The ambivalences of a bourgeois hero in an overwhelmingly middle-class society raise for him problems of estrangement and communion, sincerity and simulation, ambition and acquiescence, which we recognize as the patent themes of the great novels of the last century. The wretched fate of the lower-class hero, caught between malignant Heredity and crushing Environment in the *roman expérimental* of Zola, and in the less experimental but more benign novels of the brothers Goncourt, reflects the familiar bias of Naturalism and marks a further stage in the disintegration of heroism. Victim to immitigable "cosmic laws," with little or no control over his fate in the world, man turns inward again.

. . . .

With the retrenchment of the individual, the drama of good and evil which the hero and villain once objectified in society becomes blurred. The traditional forms of moral conflict are so internalized that no victory or defeat, where self is divided against itself, can claim to be more than pyrrhic.[23]

Hassan's comments are typical of those critics who see the development of the hero in Western literature of the last two hundred years as a record of the steadily worsening relationship between the individual and society. But one must keep in mind that these characters are rebelling against what had been an established tradition dating back centuries in which the hero supported and often propagated the values of the society of which he was a part. For, when looking at Neo-Black literature, one will certainly find heroes with many of the characteristics which critics have defined as anti-heroic. Yet, the heroic tradition of Black people in this country has been, of necessity, different from and most often in opposition to the heroic tradition of the Western Europeans who have dominated the cultural and political and social life of this country.

A hero is one who is on the side of and supports his society's version of morality and/or order and/or history.[24] The Black person who comes closest—at least publicly—to the kind of ideal embodied in this definition and whom a number of Blacks may have acknowledged as a "hero," is Booker T. Washington. However, his stock has declined to the point that in many Black circles, his name —if used at all—is a synonym for Uncle Tom.

American society has, from the outset of its relationship with Blacks, placed too many obstacles in the path of Black support of the American moral values to which so much lip service is given. Slave marriages, for example, were illegal and where there is no marriage, there can be no adultery. Slaves were forced to fornicate so that the women could yield up more commodities for the auction block. A Black person who killed another during slavery was not guilty of murder but of destroying the master's property. After slavery, the killing of one Black by another was of little consequence because a "nigger" was worthless. Families were often separated and sold to different households hundreds of miles apart. Whatever the intrinsic worth of America's moral values, slavery made many of these values meaningless for the enslaved. A dual value system developed in which stealing, lying and other forms of deceit were justified by the necessity of surviving a cruel and criminal system. As Andrew Jackson said in the narrative of his life as a slave, a "lie is often so useful to them, and the truth so often disastrous, and their aptness at a lie is such, that they take in sustaining it an air of assurance and tranquillity which imposes on strangers. . . ."[25]

The moral values, standards of what is right and what is wrong, complement the social order for the order gives a formal structure to many of a society's moral values and customs. But America's legal system classified the Black man as three-fifths of a white man so that white Southerners could have a larger representation in the national congress; in all other things he was property. Property, cannot, of course, commit any crimes. After emancipation, the federal government gave Black people the thirteenth, fourteenth and fifteenth amendments to insure their full citizenship. The Southern states later enacted the Black codes and took away all that the federal government had given and then some. By obeying the slave codes and Black codes, Blacks agreed with the assumption upon which these codes were based: that Blacks, as Chief Justice Rodger B. Taney put it in 1857, had no rights which a white man need respect. It was imperative that Black people develop means of circumventing American laws, of appearing to comply with the letter, to insure their physical survival, while disobeying the sense in order to insure their spiritual survival. Heroism for Black Americans has always meant some measure of revolt against social structures, for these structures were the instruments of their oppression rather than their protection. And, a Black American who totally supports the American social and moral order or the accepted view of this country's history commands little or no respect among Black people, and may even be ostracized as Uncle Tom, Aunt Jane, or simply and coldly as House Nigger. The House Nigger is someone else's version of hero.

In order to find a Black version of a hero, one must look someplace other than the definitions proffered by Western traditions. One can find him in the character types who are immortalized in Black songs and legends, in Black fact and reality. He is the rebel leader who revolts against physical bondage, and the streetman, the hard man, the supreme game runner who survives through heart—courage—the power of his rap—his conversation—and the bossness of his front—the effectiveness of the various guises and disguises which he wears in order to manipulate others, as well as the calmness—the icy cool—with which he faces the always changing fortunes of his life. More often than not, his survival involves what white society would term guile, deceit and treachery. In Black America, it is called putting folks into tricks, running games on them or merely hustling, and Black people will applaud, admire and envy these heroes even as the heroes run games on them, put them into tricks and rebel against the rules and conventions which have proscribed the places of Blacks and whites alike in this nation.

THE HEROIC TRADITION IN BLACK AMERICA

The rebels, such as the slave revolt leaders, Nat Turner, Gabriel Prosser and Denmark Vesey, may, when viewed from today's perspective, appear to be heroes in the classic and/or American sense. Despite William Styron's meditations on history, these men have come down to Black people in legends, in historical and fictional accounts of their deeds, as men of great nobility and physical prowess. These rebels were revolting against a system which equated human beings with property, and they were asserting their right and the right of their followers to determine their own destinies, their right to be treated as men and women without the descriptive modifiers which always reduced their status to something less than that of other men and women, that is, white men and women. Both aspects are important, for while many Americans doubted the legality and morality of slavery, many of these same people also doubted the equality of Black and white. One can call both revolt leaders and abolitionists, rebels, but it is important to keep in mind the two things that motivated the revolt leaders, for not all abolitionists were guided by the same thoughts. And the point is not really whether one is a rebel, the other something else. The point is that the term rebel, in the case of the Black revolt leaders, is a synonym for hero, rather than anti-hero, for they established through their actions a heroic model and tradition based on Black necessity.

The contemporary rebels such as Martin Luther King, Jr. and Medgar Evers appear to come closer to the classic heroic model. Yet, the opposition from the dominant society which they met at every turn and the fact that each met his death while engaged in making American law *de facto*, indicates that while they were on the side of justice and law, their activities were in direct opposition to the mores and practices of this society.

The streetmen do not even approach the ideal embodied in the classic model, for their life styles, their heroic feats, are performed almost entirely within the limits of that portion of the Black experience called, by various people, "sporting life," "the cool life," "street corner life," "street life," and simply, "the Life."[26] Each label is indicative of the fact that the Life is most often viewed as a phenomenon of experience among lower-income Black people in the urban ghettos of America. Yet the characters who have gained heroic stature in the Life, the hard man or "gorilla" type exemplified by the rough fighter or strong man whose physical strength and courage make it possible for him to accept and overcome the challenges of the world, and the trickster who, like his real-life counterpart, the pimp and the con man, achieves his ends through guile and his ability with words, are traditional figures in the Black experience whether it be urban or rural. The folk heroes, Stagger Lee and the Signifyin' Monkey, posit, as Roger Abrahams notes, two distinct types of heroism, the gorilla hard man and the trickster, both of which are current in the rural and urban experiences of Black people.[27] Thus, even though the term "street life" has been used in the past to denote a life style which has come to seem exclusively urban, its connotative value, which embraces the dirt trail as well as the asphalt road, is also implied in its use in this discussion.

There are several descriptions of street life but no real definitions. It is difficult to distill out of the complex patterns of interaction which occur in the Life, a simple statement which conveys the way in which the Life touches and affects the lives of most Black people in any given community. For the Life not only comprises the pimps, dope pushers, numbers runners, gamblers, stick-up men and the "rowdies" who frequent the bars and joints and dance halls. Each church sister who plays a number with the local runner, each member of the Black bourgeoisie who buys a stolen stereo or dress or suit, each playboy—or girl—no matter what their profession or economic status, who attempts to use their sexual attractiveness as a means of manipulation and exploitation, participates in and supports the Life ethic, "Take what you can get when you can get it."[28] For the Life is not so much a class phenomenon as it is a Black phenomenon.

The apocryphal story is told of a predominantly Black college in a large urban area which had a problem with drugs being sold on campus. With the help of the local police and the local rackets' boss, the problem of professionals selling drugs on campus was brought under control. But the police, in cracking down on the illegal traffic in drugs, also cracked down on the stolen items, mostly clothing and small appliances, which were being sold on campus. The faculty, most of whom were bona fide members of the Black middle and upper-middle class in both income and attitudes and not, by any stretch of the imagination, militants or radicals who think it revolutionary to liberate the white man from his luxury items, were upset at having their ready source of cheap, barely used goods cut off. The story is probably not true. The fact that it is told at all, however, indicates the broad participation in and support of the mores and values of the Life.

As R. Lincoln Keiser points out in *The Vice Lords,* the role of streetman is one which most Black males living in the ghetto assume at one time or another.[29] In the role of streetman, one tries to "game" or manipulate another person out of as much as possible. Each game has its limits and whether one is game runner or victim, trickster or tricked, he is obligated to follow the almost intuitive rules which set limits on the way in which the game must be run.

The idealized streetman may use either the gorilla or trickster as his model. By whatever method he chooses, the streetman becomes a dream merchant and game runner who makes his living by appearing to fulfill other people's dreams. Both models have in common a code which places the highest value on "coolness," that elusive quality which means calmness in facing both the best and the worst that life has to offer. It is a distinctive and personal style which marks one as a hip person who can take care of himself without losing any of that personal flair.

If he is to get over, to make his hustle or game effective, he must have a good rap, a phat front, and an iceman's cool, and above all, he has to keep on getting up behind any disaster. That is, he must be able to pull, if not success from the jaws of defeat, at least a whole skin from the miscarriages of any of his schemes. He lives by his wits and usually at the expense of other people. This is the ideal streetman but reality, as Elliot Liebow notes of the men in his study of street corner life, *Tally's Corner*, is seldom a faithful reflection of this strong hard image.[30]

The list of streetmen and street types includes criminals, pimps, pushers, runners, etc., the exploitative playboy, con artists whose games are not exactly illegal, gamblers, musicians and certain kinds of preachers. The preacher may appear out of place in this context, but this reference is to a special kind of preacher. The man of God whose congregation provides him with the wherewithal to purchase expensive cars, clothes and women is certainly a trickster and game runner. And his congregation gives tacit approval to his activities by continuing to support him in the style to which he has become accustomed. They may even take a vicarious pride in the length of his car, the cost of his clothes and his prowess with women. Even the head shaking which may go on about his "godless" ways has a kind of affectionate air about it, for these ways, if they do nothing else, provide an exciting topic of conversation for the reverend's more sedate parishioners. Providing vicarious thrills for his audience is one of the reasons the Black community allows the streetman, whatever his guise, to exist. Thus, as long as hell and brimstone pour forth in appropriate proportions on Sunday the congregation and the preacher usually rock on together. And whatever else is the basis of the relationship between the preacher and his congregation, those who view themselves as part of the Life laud the preacher for his heavy game and admire the toughness of his front.

The Black musician who plays Black music—jazz, blues, rhythm and blues, gospels—touches the Life physically through his work in the clubs, bars, dance halls and churches of the community. Despite the fact that he is neither a game runner nor trickster—he deals in the give and take of life and is aware of his dependence on the people—he is a vital and necessary part of the Life. He is a shaman, both doctor and minister, to the people and his function is to transmute, for as long as his song lasts, all the pain and misery of his audience's existence into something with which they can come to terms or at least deal with in a manner which is more acceptable to them. The preacher may tell his congregation about life hereafter but it is the musician who tells them about life here and now. The preacher draws a line across chaos and confusion and attempts to organize that chaos by calling on a higher power. The musician organizes chaos by calling on himself and his listeners, linking their experiences together in patterns which have meaning and significance because of their commonality and universality. The spirit is with the preacher, but the people are with the musician.

Abrahams, in his study of folktales from inner-city Philadelphia, sees the trickster/hustler figure in Black folktales—and thus, by extension, the folk trickster's real-life counterpart, the game running streetman—as a veiled reaction against overdomination while preserving the role of "childish Uncle Tom," as an amoral child who, even though he does not know the difference between right and wrong, still controls the world through guile. Abrahams sees all of this as Black reaction to slavery and segregation.[31] But the Uncle Tom, as he is defined in Black culture, is not always a trickster; in fact, he is usually pictured as a cringing, servile lackey who reveres and fears the white man and who flatters him for his own gain. The theory of the trickster being no more than a reaction to slavery and segregation takes no account of the fact that the trickster plays an important role in ancient West African folklore. Cunning, Susan Feldman notes in her introduction to *African Myths and Tales*, is the prime virtue of the West African hero and the pervasive theme of African folklore is the victory of cunning over force. The African trickster is amoral, but his "amorality is not that of the anomic presocialized individual who has not yet matured to a sense of responsibility. Suave, urbane and calculating, the African trickster acts with premeditation, always in control of the situation; though self-seeking, his social sense is sufficiently developed to enable him to manipulate others to his advantage . . . [the] trickster operates in a real world where the hero cannot count on supernatural helpers, and clever cheating replaces magic."[32] Certainly, these qualities are more characteristic of John, the trickster slave, and Shine, his urban counterpart, and the Signifyin' Monkey than those qualities which Abrahams cites. The earliest records of real-life Black tricksters, the narratives of the escaped slaves, point up the connection between lore and reality and the fact that the Black trickster knowingly crashes against the conventions and wrests his own versions of right from a system which condemns his every effort toward dignity and self-assertion as moral or legal wrongs.

These facts do not of course rule out the possibility that the streetman may use some of the Tom's methods in order to run a particular game, if it involves a white man. The figure of the grinning, dancing sambo is, for the trickster, one of many disguises which he chooses to assume, knowing that the white man will not, necessarily, be fooled by this mask, but knowing also that the white man is moved by the fact that it is within his power to command this demeaning performance from a Black man. The trial record of Denmark Vesey, the slave revolt leader, provides an excellent instance of this. Gullah Jacks, one of Vesey's principal lieutenants, uses the strategy of the Tom. "When arrested and brought before the Court . . . he assumed so much ignorance and looked and acted the fool so well, that some of the Court could not believe that this was the Necromancer who was sought after." But after hearing the testimony against him, he dropped this pose and it was apparent that the slave "had been caught but not tamed."[33]

The streetman, then, is a complex character type, a figure of almost mythic proportions. His roots go back to little explored areas of slavery and African folklore. The exploits of the bad men and the tricksters form a background of legend and a mythology which stands near the center of Neo-Black literature.

Notes: Chapter 1

1. Arna Bontemps, "Introduction," *Black Thunder* (Boston: Beacon Press, 1968), p. vii.

2. Alain Locke, "The New Negro," in *Dark Symphony*, James A. Emanuel & Theodore L. Gross, eds. (New York: Free Press, 1967), p. 74.

3. James Baldwin, "Many Thousands Gone," *Notes of a Native Son* (Boston: Beacon Press, 1955), pp. 35–36.

4. Janheinz Jahn, *Neo African Literature*, trans. Oliver Coburn & Ursula Lehrburger (New York: Grove Press, 1969), p. 36.

5. Benjamin Brawley, *The Negro Genius* (New York: Dodd, Mead & Co., 1937), p. 72.

6. Sterling A. Brown, "The Negro in American Fiction," *Negro Poetry and Drama and the Negro in American Fiction* (New York: Atheneum, 1969), p. 31.

7. Charles Nichols, *Many Thousands Gone* (Bloomington: Indiana University Press, 1969), p. xiii.

8. Brown, *op. cit.*, p. 100.

9. Sylvan Barnet, *et al.*, *A Dictionary of Literary Terms* (Boston: Little, Brown & Co., 1960), p. 32.

10. Langston Hughes, "The Negro Writer and the Racial Mountain," in *Black Expression*, Addison Gayle, Jr., ed. (New York: Weybright & Talley, Inc., 1969), p. 263.

11. Locke, *op. cit.*, p. 74.

12. Rudolph Fisher, *The Walls of Jericho* (New York: Arno Press, 1969), p. 121.

13. Brawley, *op. cit.*, p. 14.

14. Aubrey Bower, quoted in Stephen Bronz, *Roots of Negro Racial Consciousness* (New York: Libra Pub., Inc., 1969), p. 84.

15. Jean Toomer, *Cane* (New York: Harper & Row, 1969), p. 21.

16. Jahn, *op. cit.*, p. 242. Jahn extends the parallel between the relationship of Shakespeare's Caliban and Prospero and that between the two opposing sides in a colonialist society (first pointed out by O. Mannoni and George Lamming) to include language as a tool which Caliban can use to free himself from Prospero's oppressive influence. Where Jahn uses Caliban, I have interpolated the word, slave; where he uses Prospero, I have interpolated, master.

17. *Funk & Wagnalls Standard College Dictionary* (New York: Funk & Wagnalls Co., 1963), p. 144.

18. The editors of *Black World*, a leading literary forum and showcase for Neo-Black writers, changed the name of the magazine from *Negro Digest* to its present title in May, 1970. While editor Hoyt Fuller gave no explicit reason for the name change, his editorial implied that "Black" is a more universal and positive designation for describing people of African descent than "Negro," and that the new name was more in keeping with the content and image of the magazine. Nathan Heard, Don L. Lee and other Neo-Black writers rarely, if ever, capitalize "Negro" and it is always used in a negative context. "Black," on the other hand, is used as a synonym for people of African descent and as an all-inclusive complimentary adjective.

19. The case involved several Fresno State College (Fresno, Calif.) Black students who were accused of detaining a college dean against his will and verbally abusing him. In college disciplinary hearings, they were acquitted of verbal abuse because of the ambiguity of certain "abusive" terms in Black culture. Fresno State College *Daily Collegian*, April 17–24, 1970.

20. Barnet, *op. cit.*, p. 69.

21. Lionel Trilling, *Freud and the Crisis of Our Culture* (Boston: Little, Brown & Co., 1955), p. 58.

22. Ihab Hassan, *Radical Innocence* (Princeton, N. J.: Princeton University Press, 1961), pp. 21–22.

23. Trilling, *op. cit.*, p. 58.

24. Hassan, *op. cit.*, p. 29.

25. Andrew Jackson, "Narrative and Writings of Andrew Jackson of Kentucky", quoted in Gilbert Osofsky, *Puttin On Ole Massa* (New York: Harper & Row, 1969), p. 26.

26. William McCord lists various labels in *Life Styles in the Black Ghetto*, McCord, John Howard, *et al.*, eds. (New York: W. W. Norton & Co., 1967); *see also* R. Lincoln Keiser, *The Vice Lords* (New York: Holt, Rinehart & Winston, 1969), and Roger Abrahams, *Deep Down in the Jungle*, 1st revised ed. (Chicago: Aldine Pub. Co., 1970).

27. Abrahams, *op. cit.*, p. 64.

28. Elliot Liebow, *Tally's Corner: A Study of Negro Street Cornermen* (Boston: Little, Brown & Co., 1967), p. 147.

29. Keiser, *op. cit.*, p. 42.

30. Liebow, *op. cit.*, pp. 144–145.

31. Abrahams, *op. cit.*, pp. 64ff.

32. Susan Feldman, ed., *African Myths and Tales* (New York: Dell Pub. Co., 1963), pp. 13–14, 15, 17.

33. The Trial Record of Denmark Vesey [Introduction by John O. Killens] (Boston: Beacon Press, 1970), p. 31.

CHAPTER TWO

Rebel and Streetman
in Black Literature

... We wrapped ourselves in the cloak
Of his exploits: "Man, the last time it took eight
Screws to put him in the Hole." "Yeah, remember when he
Smacked the captain with his dinner tray." "He set
The record for time in the Hole—67 straight days!"
"Ol Hard Rock! man, that's one crazy nigger."
And then the jewel of a myth that Hard Rock had once bit
A screw on the thumb and poisoned him with syphilitic spit.

.   .   .   .

He had been our destroyer, the doer of things
We dreamed of doing but could not bring ourselves to do,
The fears of years, like a biting whip,
Had cut grooves too deeply across our backs.

Etheridge Knight
"Hard Rock Returns to Prison from
the Hospital for the Criminally Insane"
Poems from Prison

| I |

The rather arbitrary dates which critics have used to mark
the initiation and termination of movements and trends
in Black literature (the decade of the twenties dates the
Harlem Renaissance; the thirties and early forties dates
the so-called "protest" literature movement[1]) give little

70

indication of the continuity and thematic unity which has characterized much of Black literature, particularly fiction, during a large portion of its history. The dominant theme in Black fiction since the first novel by a Black writer was published in 1853 has been racial conflict, sometimes on a physical level, most often on a psychological or emotional level. William Wells Brown in *Clotel or the President's Daughter* (London, 1853)[2] couches this theme in terms of slavery and its attendant sordidness and tragedy. Almost a hundred years later, Richard Wright states this theme in terms of the brutalization of the emotions and the stifling of the spirit in *Native Son*; and John A. Williams, in his recent novel, *Sons of Darkness, Sons of Light* (New York, 1969), sees a resolution to racial conflict in violent confrontations in which Blacks adopt the Old Testament philosophy of an eye for an eye. *Native Son* and *Sons of Darkness* are not "new" or "modern," for each revolves around a theme which at least one critic, Irving Howe, feels is basic to what he defines as Negro or Black literature.[3] One, of course, cannot accept the limitations which Howe's definition would impose upon the literature. Yet, one can also see that the unique approaches of Wright and Williams to the agony of the racial issue as a literary theme are logical outgrowths of William Wells Brown's pedestrian and often poorly executed uses of this theme. Given the fact that the treatment of Black people in America has been largely characterized by brutality, sordidness and dehumaniza-

tion, it is an inescapable conclusion that Black literature
will be characterized by tragedy, such as that portrayed
in Brown's *Clotel* where the heroine's death is a commentary upon a racist climate which makes it almost impossible for a Black person to survive; violence, which is
for *Native Son*'s central character, Bigger Thomas, the
only valid means of expression left him by a society which
stifles all of the other natural and productive impulses;
and a smoldering resentment, which finally causes Eugene
Browning in *Sons of Darkness* to turn upon and kill the
visible instruments of oppression: all these are inherent
in the experiences of American Blacks. Thus the many
novels of early writers such as Brown, Charles Chesnutt,
Sutton Griggs, G. Langhorne Pryor and J. W. Grant,
all of whom published prior to 1920, lay a substantial
foundation for the twentieth century novelists who were
to follow them in portraying this theme, whose use was
born of the necessity of Black writers to explore the effects
of racist oppression on Black people and to posit solutions
to end that oppression.

Black writers have dealt with other themes whose primary focus is Blackness in America: passing for white,
the struggle for economic security and status, the malevo-
lent influences of the Black matriarchy, the South as a
spiritual homeland for Blacks, the conflict between materialistic status-striving and the response to others on the
level of feeling as the touchstone of value, the exoticism
of rural and urban Black people, and so on. However, it

is racial conflict and its many variations and ramifications which has been the dominant theme in nineteenth and twentieth century Black literature. The Black rebel leader as a heroic figure is only a minor counterpoint within this thematic framework, but his importance transcends the limited attention he has received. Indeed, the first heroes in Black literature were rebels, warriors, leaders in struggles to overthrow the more oppressive elements of white society. This is not surprising for when one begins to talk of Black heroes, it must always be in some kind of radical term.

Blake or the Huts of America (1859), a novel by Martin Delany which survives in fragment form, *Imperium in Imperio* (1899) by Sutton Griggs and *The Quest of the Silver Fleece* (1911) by W.E.B. Du Bois have heroes who rebel against the political and economic chains which hold Black people in bondage. The novels form a tentative tradition, in literature at least, of rebellion. Except for Delany's fragment which deals with an attempted slave revolt, these novels deal with the formation of Utopian states where race is no longer a point of contention. *Dark Princess* (1928) by Du Bois unites Asians and Africans in an attempt to liberate the dark people of the world from the yoke of white rule and oppression. In "Bright and Morning Star" (from the short story collection *Uncle Tom's Children*, 1936), Richard Wright creates a rebel leader, a communist organizer in the rural South, who seeks to unite Black and white workers under the banner of interracial and international brotherhood. Arna Bontemps, in *Black Thunder* (1936) and again in *Drums at Dusk* (1939), tells the story of actual slave revolts; one, *Black Thunder*, deals with the aborted slave rebellion of Gabriel Prosser in 1803; the other is a fictionalized account of the Haitian slave revolt which created a nation.

With the publication of *Native Son* in 1940, Richard Wright turned the impulse to protest in another direction. Rather than showing whites and Blacks what could happen with the help of a strong Black leader, he begins the trend in Black literature whose chief characteristic is its fierce indictment of American society because of the society's brutalizing effect on Black people. Wright and his followers and imitators "protested," as did many other Black writers, against a coercive and racist environment. To label them "protest novelists," however, is to cast a pejorative light on the writers who precede Wright and those who come after him and to limit, unfairly, the range of Wright's own artistry. Most art is, after all, a form of protest against the injustices, the indignities, the cruelties, the uglinesses of life, whether they are perpetrated by whites against Blacks or by fate or God against humanity.

It may seem surprising that Bigger Thomas is not included in the list of rebel heroes, for Margolies credits Bigger with being a "metaphysical revolutionary," Cleaver calls him "a Black rebel of the ghetto" and his creator speaks often of Bigger's "revolt."[4] Bigger is an

aborted hustler, a boy too out of touch with himself to
understand the yearnings of his own heart, too alienated
from his people and their past to find a way of bridging
the gap between the rural, religion-haunted South of his
family and the seemingly traditionless North. The murders which he commits, the first the inadvertent killing of
the rich white girl whose parents employ him as a chauf-
feur, and the second, the deliberate murder of his Black
girl friend, Bessie, are interpreted as rebellious acts
whose origins lie in the frustration engendered by the
systematic exclusion of Blacks from equal participation
in American society. And because Bigger finally breaks
through the wall of frustration which has made inarticulate all the longings and desires raging inside of him,
and is finally able to give voice to these longings in violence, critics, such as Robert Bone, have applauded his
actions.[5] But the nature of his crimes makes suspect the
idea that he has expressed anything. Bigger kills Mary
accidentally and the macabre method he uses to hide his
crime, hacking the girl's body apart and hiding the pieces,
stems more from panic than deliberate reasoning. It is
only later that calmer reflection shows him a way of
capitalizing on his crime. He tries to extort money from
the girl's parents who have not yet found her body and
believe her kidnapped. This killing is viewed as the liberating action; Bigger breaks free of the stagnant existence
in which his family and friends are held. Yet Bigger's
next action is to murder Bessie. This crime is deliberate.

There is only a difference in degree, rather than kind, between this and the other violent crimes which Black people commit against each other in most Black communities any Saturday night in the year. Had the intention behind the crimes been reversed, the white girl's death a deliberate murder and Bessie's an accident, there would be no need to modify the "revolutionary" aspect of Bigger's character with "metaphysical" or other inactive kinds of adjectives. Another important aspect of Bigger's exclusion from the ranks of rebels in the present context is that none of the people involved in the story see Bigger in this light or his actions from this point of reference. Neither his friends nor his family nor the white lawyer, Max, see Bigger as anything more than a boy who has become entangled in a series of destructive actions. Max and Jan, Mary's white boyfriend, see more penetrating reasons for Bigger's actions and see their relationship to the larger society. The other aspect, if it is there, is lost on them. Bigger remains just as alienated in the end as he was in the beginning and in this he is more akin to anti-heroes in Western literature than to the rebel leader tradition in Black literature. It is obvious that Wright was after something different, that he was not attempting to create a "Black revolutionary," but as he himself has said,

He [Bigger] was an American, because he was a native son; but he was also a Negro nationalist in a vague sense because he was not allowed to live as an American.

REBEL & STREETMAN IN BLACK LITERATURE

... his hate had placed him like a wild animal at bay, in a position where he was most symbolic and explainable. In other words, his nationalist complex was for me a concept through which I could grasp more of the total meaning of his life than I could in any other way. I tried to approach Bigger's *snarled* and *confused* nationalist feelings with *conscious* and *informed* ones of my own. Yet Bigger was not nationalist enough to feel the need of religion or the folk culture of his own people. What made Bigger's social consciousness most complex was the fact that he was hovering unwanted between two worlds—between powerful America and his own stunted place in life. ... The most that I could say of Bigger was that he felt the need for a whole life and *acted* out that need; that was all.[6]

When one compares the character of Bigger with that of Gabriel in *Black Thunder* or Bles in the *Quest of the Silver Fleece*, it is obvious that Wright's own emphasis on the confused and tangled quality of Bigger's "nationalist" feelings places this character in a category somewhat removed from these "conscious" and "informed" men whose minds are set very firmly on liberation.

The rebel hero does not play a large part in the Black literature of the forties and fifties. He reappears, however, in the sixties in John O. Killens' *And Then We Heard the Thunder*, in which the hero is driven by the racism he encounters in the segregated army, into leading a race riot among soldiers in World War II Australia. The hero in Sam Greenlee's *The Spook Who Sat by the Door* coldly and calculatingly starts "The Revolution."[7] Jacob Blue is the congressional candidate-rebel in *Black Jacob* (1969) by William Mahoney. The rebel-like overtones are muted but still present in *Sons of Darkness, Sons of Light* by John A. Williams, in which the hero precipitates interracial fighting by his retaliation against the white policeman murder of a young Black boy.

The most important and possibly the best of the rebel leader novels is Arna Bontemps' *Black Thunder*. Bontemps describes Gabriel, the slave leader, as a strong forceful Black man, unafraid of dying for his freedom and the freedom of his fellow slaves. This characterization is important, as is the fact that Gabriel's exploits are based on history. Portraying a man who "had, by his own dignity and by the esteem in which he was held, inspired and maintained loyalty," thus becoming the catalyst for the "self-assertion by Black men whose endurance was strained to the breaking point,"[8] and making the exploits of these men available to present and future generations are important functions of the novel. Had Bontemps stopped there, he would still have made a significant contribution to Black people.

But *Black Thunder* is, in addition, the story of a revolt by field slaves whose speech is a function of what they are: uneducated slaves who believe in their own humanity and who are quite capable of analyzing their situations and thinking up solutions to their problems in the speech which whites have described as "poor" English, lacking descriptive or analytic power. One cannot emphasize too much the fact that Gabriel and his followers speak dialect and that the narrator's voice at no time condescends to or patronizes them for their "non-standard" speech. Up to this point in Black literature, dialect had been used almost exclusively for caricature of Black people. Any initiative or analytic abilities shown by the dialect speaker were a result of "guile" or "craft" rather than a reflective or conscious conceptualization on the part of the speaker.

Even in the writings of Claude McKay and many other Harlem Renaissance writers who, theoretically, were glorifying the folk life of Black people, dialect-speaking characters are seldom used to embody or portray serious themes. In *Home to Harlem,* Jake speaks dialect. And, precisely because he is elemental, instinctual, even crafty if necessary, Jake is incapable of analyzing or even reflecting on his life. It is left to the character of college-bred, articulate Ray to do this. The judgment against the folk which McKay would glorify is subtle, yet implicit. Contrasting McKay's work with that of Sterling Brown and Langston Hughes, who were writing during the same time, makes the distinction clearer. Brown and Hughes used the patterns and vocabularies of folk speech, its rich imagistic and metaphorical qualities to describe, analyze and make serious, profound statements about Black life and the human condition.

In the context of the rebel and his follower, it is obvious that speech makes a big difference. If one speaks standard English, one is intelligent, an intellectual whose mature judgment and incisive mind is needed to guide a childlike people out of bondage. If one speaks dialect, one is incapable of leadership, which requires more than brute force to accomplish its objective. But Gabriel of *Black Thunder* breaks this mold and emerges as a leader, a rebel hero who is truly of the folk. He rebels not only against the physical oppression represented by his chains, but against the psychological oppression represented by the need to conform to a value system established by white men.

Bontemps and Hughes and Brown point the way to a time when Black speech is respected and savored, when all the metaphors and similes, all of the odd pronunciations which created new words and which were religiously erased from the speech of upwardly mobile Black people, are prized and pointed to as proof of Black articulation, as proof of a different and definite life style which commands respect in a pluralistic society.

| II |

The history of the streetman in Black literature is shorter and more sporadic than that of the rebel hero. The narratives of escaped and freed slaves describe some of the games—the ruses and disguises—which slaves were forced to adopt in order to survive and escape the dehumanization of slavery.[9] Street life and the streetman assume a greater importance in Black literature during the late twenties, the so-called Harlem Renaissance. The Life, in the works of many writers, was portrayed as a kind of perpetual party; everything connected with the Life took on a kind of primeval glamour because it appeared to be a free and easy mode of living which set its own standards and named its own directions. Often those standards and directions were in direct opposition to those dictated by white society. Participating in the Life, even on a vicarious level, became a form of rebellion, just as depicting it in a positive manner in literature was a form of rebellion for the writers. There are many subtleties in these characterizations of the Life; the wholehearted acceptance of street life which appears on the surface of many of these works is sometimes belied by a closer reading of them.

George Schuyler and Countee Cullen create comic but valid representations of streetmen in *Black No More* (1931) and *One Way to Heaven* (1932). The satiric *Black No More* presents a master game, a masterpiece of deception, for the plot turns upon the discovery of a cure for racial oppression: a medical process, trade named, Black No More, which turns Black people into whites. The cure has two flaws however; it does not affect the genes and the newborn children of the newly converted whites must undergo the whitening treatment. It is also discovered, near the end of the novel, that the converted whites are actually a shade whiter than the real whites, and tan becomes the "in" skin color. This knowledge, of course, provides a whole new basis for the racists who had been balked of their quarry and the novel closes with the world once more happily enmeshed in its racist pursuits.

The novel is also the story of a game within this larger game. The central character, Max Disher, having been cured of blackness, joins the Knights of Nordica, a Klan-like organization whose leaders have parlayed racial antagonisms into a fortune. With the advent of Black No More, they see their power and financial success begin to ebb. Max shows them how to use the issue of converted whites for success, power and money exceeding their wildest dreams. Max crowns this deception by marrying Helen, the daughter of the exalted ruler of the Knights. At the peak of his success, Helen becomes pregnant and Max lives in fear that the child will be born black. His fears are realized, but the doctor who delivers the baby offers to "get rid" of the child. Max is torn between his desire for a child, his knowledge that he must face the same decision each time Helen gets pregnant and the realization that the life of this baby will mean the loss of all he has worked so hard to gain. At the moment when he must finally voice his decision, Max learns that his father-in-law, the exalted ruler, and therefore Helen, is of Black ancestry. Helen, believing that the baby's color is due to her own long forgotten ancestry, pleads with Max to forgive her for having brought such embarrassment and shame upon him. Max magnanimously confesses his own parentage. His confession is of small consequence, however, for Helen has learned that color is unimportant beside the knowledge that Max loves her.

There is a coldness at the center of this comic treatment of the streetman. Max confesses at a strategic moment, for within the emotion-charged atmosphere of the confession-exposé scene his confession has the appearance of an attempt to make his wife feel better about her own loss of status. At this point in his game, Max has nothing to lose. More than half of the "real" whites in the country have been exposed as mixed bloods, and he is, therefore, in good company. Nor can Helen reproach him for having kept his ancestry secret, for she has unwittingly been guilty of the same omission.

Akin to this satiric treatment of the streetman is Cullen's comic portrayal of Sam Lucas, the continual convert in *One Way to Heaven*. Sam Lucas' way of life is one long hustle. He is a professional convert, traveling from revival meeting to revival meeting, allowing the Lord and the devil to battle for his soul, with the Lord always winning. Inspired by the drama of the conversion and sympathetic because Sam has only one arm, the congregation, in Christian charity, gives him a few dollars to help him out. Sam appears to be a romanticized version of the hustler, for Cullen portrays him as basically decent, basically good, despite his deceptions, his desertion of his wife and his philandering. He has, however, the basic hardness necessary for an efficient game runner. Bilking gullible Christians, especially impoverished Black Christians, is funny, but also rather cruel. Yet Sam does it very well and apparently without a twinge of conscience. This hardness allows him to make a death bed conversion for the benefit of his wife, Mattie (he returns to her only when he is desperately ill and in need of care). And, though one critic would have the reader believe that this is a pure impulse and therefore makes the pretense real, the conversion lacks meaning.[10] Mattie has no more touched Sam's soul or his life on his death bed than she has on their wedding day. He gives her something which has no value for him, which costs him nothing. He remains a game runner to the end.

For Richard Wright, street life is something to despair over; it combines with the racist aspects of American culture to produce embittered, dangerous men who eventually choke on their own rage. Bigger Thomas is, in part, a representative of "bad niggers," men who like Hard Rock in Etheridge Knight's poem, "Hard Rock Returns to Prison . . ." "take no shit from nobody."[11] These are hard men-gorillas, for they use their anger to manipulate whites and other Blacks and thus find a measure of freedom in crashing against the conventions which circumscribe their lives. Bigger, quite obviously, falls short of the idealization of this character type. This aspect of his character has interest for Wright only in so far as it emphasizes the victimization and brutalization of Blacks by the dominant society.

The parasitic aspect of the streetman is one of the themes of *Howard Street* (1968) by Nathan C. Heard, in which Hip, the central character, dope addict and pimp, is committed only to himself and his own survival. *How-*

ard Street is similar in its vision of the street life to Wright's *Native Son*, Ann Petry's *The Street* (1946) and Julian Mayfield's *The Hit* (1957), or any of Chester Himes's novels about the adventures of Coffin Ed and Grave Digger Jones. All seem to view the Life as a kind of vicious octopus squeezing the soul out of the Black community or turning in and devouring itself. Yet these novels are running counter to what appears to be another trend in Black literature. The game runner and the street life are emerging in Neo-Black fiction as a source of strength and power for the Black community, perhaps the last refuge against the annihilating forces of white America.

As Don L. Lee, the young militant poet, says:

. . . my heroes were the pimps, prostitutes and wineheads. I mean, at my level of consciousness, they were the strongest Black people in the community; and that strength allowed them and me to survive. They moved through the world with a bit of their humanism still intact . . . their struggle/existence was both positive and negative. Positive: they defied what was/is authority; most important, they stood up for what they considered/believed to be right. Negative: their mere actions as pimps, prostitutes and wineheads were, in fact, a very subtle way of killing themselves—physically, mentally, as well as spiritually.[12]

For most Black people and writers, the list of street heroes also includes the musician. The Life provides a Black context and writers are exploring it along with the positive and negative values of the streetman. Their characters reflect a position which embodies the defiance of the Life without its crippling alienation and egocentricity. Poets such as Lethonia Gee, David Henderson and Walt Delegall have begun to explore the tensions in the lives of musicians and the responses of Black people to them. The novelists have begun to explore the terrain of these and other streetmen. William Melvin Kelley (*A Drop of Patience*, 1965), Amiri Baraka ("The Screamers," 1960), James Baldwin (*Another Country*, 1962) bring their vision to bear on the musician. Robert Dean Pharr (*The Book of Numbers*, 1969), Clarence Major (*All-Night Visitors*, 1969) and Ernest Gaines (*Of Love and Dust*, 1968) focus on the streetman in his various guises. In this, the younger writers are extending and further developing the character type first portrayed by Schulyer and Cullen and most memorably by Ralph Ellison in *Invisible Man*.

The genial game runners of Schulyer and Cullen appear as children beside Ellison's streetman, Rinehart, that elusive character who is pimp, preacher, lover, numbers runner and rowdie in the same neighborhood and, apparently, all in the same day. Rinehart is the truest philosophical flowering of the game runner in his natural environment, the Life. Rinehart, Ellison notes, "has lived so long with chaos that he knows how to manipulate it."[13] Through Rinehart, the protagonist realizes that his world, like that of Rine the runner, is one of possibilities, that the only boundaries or limits are those which he, himself, sets. Invisibility makes possibility possible, and it is this which Rinehart takes advantage of. The protagonist only comes into contact with Rinehart through the latter's fronts. He sees only the Rine, and the heart—if there is one—remains, like the protagonist of the novel, invisible. And perhaps this is the truest description of the game runner, that his heart remains invisible, untouched; that while he may be hero, providing vicarious thrills for his public, he is more a parasite than anything else, preying on the body which feeds him, giving sham coin, transitory joy in return.

This is the posture which the protagonist rejects, yet his rejection is not negative for he also arrives at a new level of consciousness because of his exposure to the "I"-centered freedom which streetmen achieve in society. Thus, aside from being linked together by a common subject matter, writers such as Baldwin, Ellison and Gaines are also linked by a common vision which sees the streetman as an object of respect because of his hardness, his lack of fear, but only as a heroic figure, a person worthy of love, when he realizes that the world cannot be structured at the expense of others for his pleasure alone. His lone-wolf posture is called into question, for he is asked to be a part of the group as well as an individual, asked to accept love as well as take it.

This is an important point for there are obvious similarities between the streetmen in contemporary Black literature and the rogues and picaros of European and American literature. The difference can be illustrated by a brief examination of *Invisible Man* as a picaresque novel. Ellison's use of the picaresque mode—the episodic, accident-laden plot whose violently rushing events alternate between good and bad fortune, symbolizing the world's chaos[14]—as a means of structuring the protagonist's adventures is an organic necessity of his subject matter. As the early slave narratives indicate, the lives of Black people since first touching American shores have been charged with the chaotic flux engendered by the theft of family, history and culture during their forced transportation from Africa to the New World. Thus, in an extended sense, the hero's origins, as with the traditional picaresque hero, are unknown. For all intents and purposes, his history begins with his grandparents; the family history prior to them is shrouded in the mystery of slavery. The mystery of the hero's origins becomes a metaphor of his future character. The implicit uncertainty about his family history foreshadows his uncertainty about his own identity. His very namelessness throughout the novel is a function of his lack of identity. The Muslims call it not knowing one's true, that is African, or original name, or bearing the slave master's name; either expression is indicative of the fact that the family name of Black Americans is shrouded in the same mystery which hides so much of their past origins. This element is emphasized in Chapter 17 when the hero and Clifton, his Black colleague in the Brotherhood, are accosted by Ras the Exhorter, a fiery Black nationalist who angrily questions the young men's allegiance to the white-dominated and white-oriented Brotherhood:

You black and beautiful—don't let 'em tell you different! [Ras tells Clifton, who has struck him] You wasn't them t'ings you be dead, mahn. Dead! I'd have killed you, mahn. Ras the Exhorter raised his knife and tried to do it, but he could not do it. Why don't you do it? I ask myself. I will do it now, I say; but somet'ing tell me, "No, no! *You might be killing your black king!*" And I say yas, yas! [Emphasis added.][15]

Ras's uncertainty stays his hand and perhaps saves Clifton's life. But this particular uncertainty can never really be clarified and one of the minor themes of the novel is that the hero, the Black man, must deal with, must relate to those parts of his history which he can salvage and redeem even as he moves within the present.

The other picaresque characteristics which Stuart Miller cites in *The Picaresque Novel* are manifested by the protagonist in varying degrees.[16] The hero's loneliness is patent, the only relationships with a semblance of warmth or humanity are those he forms with Mary Rambo, who supports him both physically and emotionally after his abortive experience in the paint factory, and Brother Tarp who cleans up the Brotherhood offices. The protagonist's friendship with Clifton appears to have meaning and significance for him more because of what he learns from Clifton in terms of his own expanding consciousness than because the friendship has filled some emotional need. The relationships with Mary and Brother Tarp, however, are of a different order. The hero fails to achieve a deep sustained relationship with Mary even though she is the embodiment of much that is warm and giving, strong and stable in Black tradition. This is not as contradictory as it may seem, for while on the one hand the Black experience has been subjected to chaotic influences, it has also been characterized by a basic internal stability which is indicated by a continuing tradition and patterns of interaction. These have made it possible for Blacks to survive and to transcend the terrifying experience of becoming American. This is what the spirituals and the blues and jazz are about, the internal stability which makes it possible to structure the outward chaos. Mary partakes of this internal stability; it allows her to support and encourage the hero. But she cannot give him stability. He must acquire that himself.

In a similar vein, Brother Tarp, whom the hero takes little notice of until this elderly Brother gives him a link from the chain which he broke in escaping from a Southern chain gang, embodies the ultimate stability of Black tradition. The link of chain is, as George Kent states, "Symbolically, . . . a bitter link in the chain of Black tradition."[17] But the fact that Brother Tarp is alive and able to pass it on to the hero, also symbolizes endurance and transcendence of that bitter experience. The chain link must therefore stand with Mary's minstrel bank as memories at once historical and modern which must be integrated into a meaningful future. Brother Tarp and

Mary can only give the hero what Lawrence J. Clipper would, perhaps, characterize as "amulets" and "charms" and the "spell" of their experiences as supportive devices;[18] his increasingly broadened understanding must help him to utilize them and thus achieve for himself an inner stability. These two approaches to warmth and spontaneity in human relationships underscore the hero's lack of internal stability, a lack which is also characteristic of the picaro.

The protean quality of the hero is obvious. He moves from the role of college student to factory worker to political organizer to that of aborted trickster. His one conscious attempt at deception, when he attempts to follow his grandfather's advice on how to deal with the white man, that is, "I want you to overcome 'em with yeses, undermine 'em with grins, agree 'em to death and destruction, let 'em swoller you till they vomit or burst wide open," ends in disaster for him and for the Black community he wants to help. The protean aspect of his nature is objectified when he consciously assumes a disguise, sunglasses and a big stetson hat, in order to escape the vengeance of Ras prior to the riot which engulfs Harlem. Clifton moves from political organizer to vendor of sambo dolls (which, as symbols, take their place beside the minstrel bank and the chain link); during the riot, Ras the Exhorter becomes Ras the Destroyer. These role changes and those of the hero are indicative of changing fortunes, the chaotic world, but also of an expanding and changing consciousness which demands that roles and actions be adjusted to new visions of reality.

The most significant divergence from the traditional picaro pattern lies in the hero's education. Miller would have one believe that the protagonist "is taught by the world to be a rogue; . . . he begins to embrace trickery for its own sake or as a protest against the nature of the world's disorder."[19] Even the most superficial reading of the novel belies this contention, for while the hero is certainly taught that one can make it through the world as a rogue—his experiences with Bledsoe, the president of the Black college, and Brother Jack, one of the leaders of the Brotherhood, are proof of this—his one attempt at trickery, roguery, fails. Rather than embracing trickery, he in fact turns away from it, a rejection which is symbolized by his rejection of Rinehart and his methods. As he says in the Epilogue, ". . . what do *I* really want. . . . Certainly not the freedom of Rinehart or the power of a Jack, nor simply the freedom not to run." The roots of this rejection lie in the ideal relationship between the Black man and Black tradition and are just as organic to the novel as its picaresque structure.

The model for this kind of relationship is the call and response pattern which plays such a large part in Black music and the almost ritualistic word games of street life. The individual defines himself, sometimes against, but always because of, the group experience which provides the frame of reference. The interplay between individual personality and the group is neither so rigidly structured that individual expression is stifled, nor so formless that the individual can forget that his roots are in the group, that to tear himself away from them is to stop up his heart's blood. This interplay is like that which goes on in the call and response pattern between a lead singer and a choir, between a holiness preacher and his congregation when the preaching gets good and they all have the Spirit. It is the kind of relationship which exists in jazz groups where, as Ellison describes it, a "delicate balance is struck between strong individual personality and the group . . ."[20]

Gene Bluestein, in his article, "The Blues as a Literary Theme," sees this relationship in *Invisible Man*, but only as an indirect theme.[21] The pattern underlies the structure of the novel, however, and emerges in the prologue to the book when the protagonist, helped along by a little marijuana, descends into the depths of Louis Armstrong's version of "Black and Blue":

And *beneath the swiftness of the hot tempo there was a slower tempo and a cave and I entered it and looked around and heard an old woman singing a spiritual as full of Weltschmerz as flamenco, and beneath that lay a still lower level on which I saw a beautiful girl the color of ivory pleading in a voice like my mother's as she stood before a group of slave owners who bid for her naked body, and below that I found a lower level and a more rapid tempo and I heard someone shout:*

"Brothers and sisters, my text this morning is the 'Blackness of Blackness.'"

And a congregation of voices answered: "That blackness is most black, brother, most black . . ."

GIVE BIRTH TO BRIGHTNESS

The protagonist is descending through space and time and history, back through one of the first Americanized responses of Black people to this country, symbolized by the spiritual, through the union of Black and white which must have happened almost as soon as the first Black woman stepped off the first slave ship—a union which did not produce a human being but another commodity to be sold at auction—to the beginning where Black is the progenitor of all life. And at the beginning is the communal pattern of call and response, individual and group in a mutually sustaining relationship. The leader calls and the "congregation of voices" responds, repeating, adding to, defining what the lead speaker says, group and individual driving each other on to the final statement "Black will make you . . ."/"Black . . ."/". . . or black will unmake you," which the protagonist's adventure in the body of the novel confirms.

This pattern is suggested again and again, especially near the beginning of the book, each time the protagonist is confronted with a symbol of his roots. There is his encounter (Chapter 9) with the Black cartman who says, perhaps symbolically, "Hell, ain't nobody out here this morning but us colored—why you trying to deny me?" and who would lead the protagonist through a ritual word game back to his roots. The protagonist refuses to respond to the cartman's call, but he does not deny its validity. Or again, in Chapter 13, the protagonist eats, relishing every bite, the baked sweet potatoes and therefore fortifies

himself, metaphorically, to accept responsibility to and
for the old couple, to respond to the call of their eviction
from the apartment in which they have lived for years.
Mary's grinning minstrel bank and Clifton's sambo dolls
require the hero to feel, to be a part of the humanity which
the derogatory stereotypes are meant to hide. Brother
Tarp's chain link reminds him that Black people have
endured, have survived, and do, in fact, live. And only
when the hero has at last internalized the group values of
identity and humanity behind these objects and incidents
is he able to leave the physical symbols behind.

The contrast between Rinehart and the novel's protagonist is implicit. Both live in a world of "infinite
possibilities," but Rinehart has chosen to define those
possibilities solely in terms of himself. The protagonist,
however, sees his possibilities in terms of a "socially responsible role." He rejects the Rinehart role because it is
a life style which draws its sustenance from the group but
gives nothing of lasting worth in return. Thus, at its core,
the education of *Invisible Man*'s Westernized picaro is
not to the values of roguery, to the parasitic role of trickster, but to the values of community and social responsibility, of Black tradition and heritage. As the game
running hero of *The Life and Loves of Mr. Jiveass Nigger*
says of the Black expatriates in Copenhagen:

[They all] seem to be living off someone or something else.
Everything but their insides. . . . [Their hustling is] only an
excuse for not being able to live off their *insides* . . . if you're

black you don't need to get at anything. You're already there. You can live right out of your insides.[22]

One's insides, the group experience which one internalizes and one's own experience which one lives, is all that a Black man needs, all in fact that he can rely on in his struggle to remain human in the white man's world. The interplay of the two provides the necessary support so that one is able to withstand the attempts at dehumanization and emasculation.

Thus, to view the streetman wholly within the context of the Western picaresque tradition is to obscure significant aspects of the streetman's portrayal in contemporary Black literature. For it is not the individual versus the group—a confrontation where one must necessarily be the taker, the other the taken—to which Ellison and the Neo-Black writers would recall the streetman, but to the individual *and* the group where one provides a communal frame, a Black context, within which the other can achieve his personal vision enriched by a sense of community and tradition.

Notes: Chapter 2

1. See, for example, Robert Bone, *The Negro Novel in America*, Rev. ed. (New Haven: Yale University Press, 1965) ; Stephen H. Bronz, *Roots of Negro Racial Consciousness* (New York: Libra Pub. Inc., 1964) & the previously cited Jahn and Margolies.

2. The versions which Brown revised for American readers and

issued between 1860–1867 differed from their British predecessor; the mulatto heroine was no longer the illegitimate daughter of Thomas Jefferson but the illegitimate daughter of a rich Southern planter. She is united with her Black rebel lover and reunited with her guilt-stricken father at the novel's end. For a reconstruction of the plots of the several versions, see, Jean F. Yellin's preface to *Clotel or the President's Daughter* (New York: Arno Press & The New York Times, 1969).

3. Irving Howe, "Black Boys and Native Sons," *A World More Attractive* (New York: Horizon Press, 1963), pp. 99–100. "What . . . was the experience of a man with a Black skin, what *could* it be in this country? How could a Negro put pen to paper, how could he so much as think or breathe, without some impulsion to protest, be it harsh or mild, political or private, released or buried? The 'sociology' of his existence formed a constant pressure on his literary work, and not merely in the way this might be true for any writer, but with a pain and ferocity that nothing could remove."

4. Richard Wright, "How 'Bigger' Was Born," *Native Son* (New York: Harper & Row, 1940); Margolies, *op. cit.*, p. 82; Cleaver, *op. cit.*, p. 106.

5. Bone, *op. cit.*, p. 146.

6. Wright, *op. cit.*, p. xxiv.

7. In the vocabulary of many American Black nationalists, there is only one revolution: the one which will free Blacks and the oppressed majority of the world from the yoke of European domination and exploitation.

8. Arna Bontemps, "Introduction," *Black Thunder* (Boston: Beacon Press, 1968), pp. xii–xiii, xv.

9. Charles Nichols, *Many Thousands Gone*, gives an excellent summary and analysis of the published narratives of freed and escaped slaves.

10. Bone, *op. cit.*, p. 79.

11. Etheridge Knight, "Hard Rock Returns to Prison from the Hospital for the Criminally Insane," *Poems from Prison* (Detroit: Broadside Press, 1968), p. 11.

12. Don L. Lee, "Notes from a Black Journal," *Negro Digest*, XIX (Jan. 1970), p. 85.

13. Ralph Ellison, "The Art of Fiction: An Interview," *Shadow and Act* (New York: New American Library, 1964), p. 181.

14. Stuart Miller, *The Picaresque Novel* (Cleveland: Case Western Reserve University Press, 1967), p. 44.

15. Ralph Ellison, *Invisible Man* (New York: New American Library, 1952), p. 324.

16. Uncertain origins, inability to love, internal instability, education to roguishness and trickery and protean roles are generally considered the primary characteristics of the picaro.

17. George E. Kent, "Ralph Ellison and Afro-American Folk and Cultural Tradition," *CLA Journal*, XIII (March 1970), p. 273.

18. Lawrence J. Clipper, "Folklore and Mythic Elements in *Invisible Man*," *CLA Journal*, XIII (March 1970), pp. 229–241.

19. Miller, *op. cit.*, p. 134.

20. Ellison, "Living With Music," *Shadow and Act*, p. 189.

21. Gene Bluestein, "The Blues as a Literary Theme," in Jules Chametzky & Sidney Kaplan, eds. *Black and White in American Culture* (Amherst: University of Mass. Press, 1969), p. 253.

22. Cecil Brown, *The Life and Loves of Mr. Jiveass Nigger* (New York: Farrar, Straus & Giroux, 1969), p. 203.

II The Renegade Disguise

| VIII |

A renegade
behind the mask. And even
the mask, a renegade
disguise. Black skin
and hanging lip.

> Lazy
> Frightened
> Thieving
> Very potent sexually
> Scars
> Generally inferior

(but natural

rhythms.
His head is at the window. The only
part
    that sings.

Amiri Baraka
from "A Poem for Willie Best"
Part VIII
The Dead Lecturer

CHAPTER THREE

The Limitations of a Middle-Class "Hero"

Where
ever,
        he has gone. Who ever
mourns
or sits silent
to remember

There is nothing of pity
here. Nothing
of sympathy.

Amiri Baraka
from "A Poem for Willie Best"
Part IV
The Dead Lecturer

| I |

Several critics have analyzed the plays of Amiri Baraka as they relate to Neo-Black drama, the Black Theatre movement. The critics have done so in the process of seeking to define what the movement is, what it should be and how Black playwrights in this movement can best help Black people achieve certain social and political aims.[1] This kind of analysis is certainly needed if future generations of Black students are not to be faced (as is the

101

present generation) with the spectacle of having to turn to white scholars who may not—and probably don't— have enough understanding of Black life and the nuances of its points of divergence from the life of whites in this country to give an authoritative account of trends in Black literature and their meaning and significance for either Blacks or whites. But a context analysis, other than that currently being done by the proponents and exponents of Neo-Black literature, is also needed. The reference here is not to the kind of chronological surveys which white critics are so fond of bringing out, in which Wright gives "birth" to Baldwin, gives birth to Ellison, gives birth to Williams, gives birth to Baraka, *ad infinitum*. This kind of survey implies that one has been the progenitor of the others and fails to give emphasis to other factors in the background of the writers which may have had more influence than their physical or psychological association with one person or institution. It is not mere chronology which provides the needed reference for Baraka or any Black writer. Rather, critics must attempt to see Black literature as it relates to and illuminates the underlying currents of Black life and must attempt to describe and define its indigenous traditions.

Baraka, more than attempting to forge a new Black language or create, as he says, new gods, is embodying within his works many currents and traditions which have made life, Black life, what it is. His work is set in many different contexts and when looked at as art, having social and political, cultural and artistic contexts, one begins to perceive the depth and scope of his work.

The plays *Dutchman* and *The Slave* are given a place in this book because they come near the end of that hybrid tradition which has influenced Black fiction since 1853. The two plays bring this tradition to a logical fruition and point toward a new direction. Baraka performs a service like that of Richard Wright two decades before. By exposing Bigger Thomas' anger—and, by extension, the anger and bitterness of Bigger's real-life counterparts—to public view, Wright made it easier for other Black writers not only to explore Black anger but to move beyond the relatively simple statement of anger to a more complex analysis of Black in relation to white. Bigger Thomas' fury is all the more terrible in its intensity because it is inarticulate. He cannot say who has messed over him or precisely how they have done it. He only knows that he has been messed with. He strikes outward in a blind instinctual movement which is violent because only through violence can he express the depth of his rage and pain. The characters in Baraka's early plays, particularly Clay and Walker, have all the fury of Bigger but it is their awareness, their ability to analyze and articulate their situation which is so terrible and shocking. Their fury and pain have been internalized to such an extent that even outward action, as in *The Slave*, brings no release and they, like Bigger, choke on their own rage. It is not without significance that *The Slave* and *Dutchman* take the physical form of dialogues or conversations between a Black man and white people, for just as Wright abstracts the message of *Native Son* by putting into the mouth of Bigger's white lawyer a long analysis of the social context of Bigger's crimes and the subsequent appeal to the white jury (white society), Baraka seeks to educate white society to the feelings and situations of the collective Black man. All three works are addressed to the collective might and power of the white man. The Black characters are stripped of tradition, culture, any identifying patterns of interaction or group experience which do not deal with a racist-engendered anger. They are not people but representative character types meant to convey specific ideas and attitudes and, while they may be illuminating for Black people (Baldwin in *Notes of a Native Son* remarks that Wright's "work was an immense liberation and revelation to me"),[2] this is a by-product of what appears to be the intended goal of reaching the minds and hearts of white people. Thus, Walker and Clay are latter-day Bigger Thomases. They are viewed, it is true, from a different perspective, but Baraka's sights are trained on the same object as Wright's. And, while there is overstatement in Charles Gordone's view that "[Baraka] has said everything there is to be said in terms of Black and white relationships,"[3] it is certain that he has exhausted by thorough exploration in these and other plays Black/white conflict as a literary theme, leaving other artists the room to explore the Black heart. And it is the Black heart, as the seat of courage, emotion, action, which is the crux of the present discussion.

| II |

Dutchman is a two-scene, two-character play of powerful dimensions and chilling implications. Ostensibly, it is the story of a young, Ivy League Black man, Clay, who allows himself to be picked up by a white woman, Lula, on a New York subway. When Clay refuses to conform to Lula's vision of the Black man as a "hip field-nigga," she taunts him into revealing his antagonism toward all whites as well as revealing the self which he hides under his Ivy League front, his façade, and then she kills him. And the audience's smug agreement with Lula's charge that Clay is nothing more than a third-rate imitation white man changes to shock and surprise as Clay reveals the awareness which looks out from behind his front.

The plot line in itself has several implications, the most important being that the survival of the Black man in America, or the Western world, for that matter, is predicated upon his ability to keep his thoughts and his true identity hidden. As Baraka himself has stated in "A Poem for Willie Best," the Black man thus becomes "A renegade/ behind the mask. And even/ the mask, a renegade/ disguise." And when one views the implicit assumption that Black people hide behind stereotyped images through the prism of the three myths embodied in the play, further dimensions are added to this theme.

The myth or legend implicit in the title "Dutchman" is that of the ghost ship, the *Flying Dutchman,* which roamed the seas and added unwary ships to its phantom entourage. As though to underline the spectral implications of the title, Baraka sets the scene for the opening of the play: "In the flying underbelly of the city. Steaming hot, summer on top, outside. Underground. The subway heaped in modern myth."[4] One does not want to push this opening statement too much, but Lula's action at the end of the play, after she has killed Clay and, with the help of the other occupants of the subway coach, thrown his body overboard, tends to confirm the supposition that Clay's death is no instance of mere feminine caprice or a random act.

Lula busies herself straightening her things. Getting everything in order. She takes out a notebook and makes a quick scribbling note. Drops it in her bag. The train apparently stops and all the others get off, leaving her alone in the coach.

Very soon a young Negro of about twenty comes into the coach with a couple of books under his arm. He sits a few seats in back of Lula. When he is seated, she turns and gives him a long slow look. He looks up from his book and drops the book on his lap.

The implication seems plain that the young Black man will be pushed into playing Clay and Lula will perform her ritual murder again. Lula is thus subtly aligned with the supernatural, the ghostly, the powers of death and destruction. She is likened to a ghost ship, cruising the city's underbelly, asking Black men the question, Which side are you on? and murdering those who, like Clay, respond, My own. One realizes that had Clay continued to hide, had he traded his Ivy League front for that of the hip field-nigga as Lula wanted, she would have allowed him to live. For it is she, as a representative of the white power structure and a symbol of the sexuality which white men have used, both as justification of Black castration and oppression and as an inducement to Black men to accept that castration, who has the power of life and death over him.

The historical dimension to the title is equally significant, for it was a Dutchman, a Dutch man-of-war, which brought the first Black slaves to North America. America symbolically comes full circle through Lula's—the *Dutchman*'s—murderous actions. The economic foundations of the nation were contained in the Dutchman's Black cargo and that cargo, as slave, freedman and would-be citizen has been the source of controversy and conflict. America's economy is no longer based on chattel slavery yet the issue of how Black people are to live and prosper continues to be a problem, a festering irritant under the nation's skin. The problems raised at Jamestown are resolved on the subway: What the Dutchman has given, the *Dutchman* also takes away.

The other occupants of the coach, sitting quietly as she leads up to her murderous finale, helping eagerly to "bury" Clay, these are Lula's crew. It is not without significance that this crew is both Black and white, that it apparently changes with each of Lula's victims. The Blacks, the Negroes, are what Lula has accused Clay of being, imitation white men with no traitorous awareness peeking from behind their various façades. The whites are the power structure of which Lula is so vocal an exponent. The crew changes, making every segment of American society a participant, if silent, in the murder of Black men.

The apples which Lula enters the subway eating so daintily at the beginning of the play seem to bear some resemblance to the biblical fruit of the tree of knowledge in Christian mythology. For, as Lula tells Clay after he has accepted an apple from her, "Eating apples is always the first step." Clay's acceptance of the apple is, presumably, the first step in his "quest" for carnal knowledge of her or at least submission to the idea of knowing her. One is tempted to ask, just where was Eden that a Black man could be tempted from it by a white woman? But it is not Eden from which Lula seeks to tempt Clay. Rather, she seeks to tempt him from behind the safe, assimilationist façade under which Baraka seems to feel Black people have sought refuge. The shared apples seem to establish the needed intimacy for Lula to metaphorically catapult Clay onto the exposed, untenable promontory from which she pushes him to his death.

But for one splendid moment he reveals not only himself but also Lula and through her the ignorance and hypocrisy of the structure which she represents; reveals that the pretense in which she wants him to join—"And we'll pretend the people cannot see you. That is, the citizens. And that you are free of your own history. And I am free of my history. We'll pretend that we are both anonymous beauties smashing along through the city's entrails" —is not lightly self-mocking or even hip. It is bogus and sinister and Clay's distant observation of it is his only possibility of salvation. And his observation of Lula and her world is distant, despite Lula's charge that Clay "crawled through the wire and made tracks to her side." But Lula assumes that Clay's front is an accurate reflection of his pumping Black heart. Hence, her plea, "Clay, you got to break out," is rather hollow and is perhaps more a plea for her own salvation than for his.

Lula is in many ways the prototype of the white hipster who presumes to know Black people and their culture better than Black people know it themselves. It is her insistence that Clay conform to her view of him which brings about the outburst which leads to his death. As she says early in the play, lying helps her to control the world. This particular lie is what Lorraine Hansberry has called the image of the "eternal exotic,"[5] another of the images which Blacks have hidden behind in order to survive and which whites have promoted, have in fact gloried in, in order not to see the humanity of Black people. To see that humanity is to confront their own guilt. Clay strips aside his "renegade mask" and the violent Black heart is illuminated:

You telling me what I ought to do. (*Sudden scream frightening the whole coach*) Well, don't! Don't tell me anything. If I'm a middle class fake white man . . . let me be. And let me be in the way I want. (*Through his teeth*) . . . Let me be who I feel like being. Uncle Tom. Thomas. Whoever. It's none of your business. You don't know anything except what's there for you to see. An act. Lies. Device. Not the pure heart, the pumping black heart. You don't ever know that. And I sit here in this buttoned-up suit to keep myself from cutting all your throats. I mean wantonly. You great liberated whore! You fuck some black man, and right away you're an expert on black people. What a lotta shit that is. The only thing you know is that you come if he bangs you hard enough. And that's all. . . . Old bald-headed four-eyed ofays popping their fingers . . . and don't even know yet what they're doing. They say, "I love Bessie Smith." And don't even understand that Bessie Smith is saying "Kiss my ass. Kiss my black unruly ass." Before love, suffering, desire, anything you can explain, she's saying, and very plainly, "Kiss my black ass." And if you don't know that, it's you that's doing the kissing.

The world in which Clay moves is revealed as a shadowy world filled with images and illusions, where one's true self, one's true identity is hidden, revealed to members only, where manhood is a secret between a man and his horn or a man and his Ivy League suit, and image and illusion, horn and suit form a barrier against the sanity which can only bring death. As Clay says of Charlie Parker:

Charlie Parker? Charlie Parker. All the hip white boys scream for Bird. And Bird saying, "Up your ass feeble-minded ofay! Up your ass." And they sit there talking about the tortured genius of Charlie Parker. Bird would've played not a note of music if he just walked up to East Sixty-seventh Street and killed the first ten white people he saw. Not a note! And I'm the great would-be poet. Yes. That's right. Poet. Some kind of bastard literature . . . all it needs is a simple knife thrust. Just let me bleed you, you loud whore, and one poem vanished. A whole people of neurotics, struggling to keep from being sane. And the only thing that would cure the neurosis would be your murder. Simple as that. I mean if I murdered you, then other white people would understand me. You understand? No. I guess not. . . . All of them. Crazy niggers turning their backs on sanity. When all it needs is that simple act. Murder. Just murder! Would make us all sane.

The central concern of the play is not identity as one knows it from contemporary literature. For Clay's whole life is predicated upon the conscious effort of hiding what he knows is his own Black self from his eyes and the eyes of others. Rather, the concern is with a denial, not only of identity, but of heroism. As Clay says, "[I'd] rather be a fool. . . . Safe with my words and no deaths and clean, hard thoughts urging me to new conquests." Black heroism for Clay would be a clear rational solution for white pollution, for the "hurt the white man has put on the people . . ."[6] He prophesies the time when whites will be caught in their own trick, be victimized by their own game:

Tell him [Lula's father] not to preach so much rationalism and cold logic to these niggers. Let them alone. . . . Don't make the mistake, through some irresponsible surge of Christian charity, of talking too much about the advantages of Western rationalism, or the great intellectual legacy of the white man, or maybe they'll begin to listen. . . . And on that day, as sure as shit, when you really believe you can "accept" them into your fold, as half-white trustees late of subject peoples . . . all of those ex-coons will be stand-up Western men, with eyes for clean hard useful lives, sober, pious and sane, and they'll murder you. They'll murder you, and have very rational explanations. Very much like your own. They'll cut your throats, and drag you out to the edge of your cities so the flesh can fall away from your bones, in sanitary isolation.

But he backs away from this vision, tries to climb back into his buttoned-up suit, collect his books and get off the train in which he has journeyed in time as well as space. His retreat from participation in this solution is again a denial of his identity. But once having shown himself to the white world, he learns that there is no retreat and he becomes just another dead nigger.

| III |

As just another dead nigger, Clay takes his place in a long line of fallen Black males who believed that the solution to their Negro problem was for Black people to be less Negro. He is heir to the tradition which Robert Bone calls assimilationism, and while one may question Bone's qualification as an expert on Black traditions and the psychological workings of Black authors, his "theoretical concepts of assimilationism and Negro nationalism"[7] appear to be attempts to define and describe a kind of public dialogue among Black intellectuals and race leaders which has been going on since the beginning of the nineteenth century. The goal of ending oppression for all Blacks, whether that oppression be slavery, as was the case in the nineteenth century slave narratives, or political, social and economic oppression, as in the post-Reconstruction South, Bone characterizes as "Negro nationalism." Assimilationism seems to mean that one accepts the various stereotypes which bolster the white supremacist's image on a group basis while one rejects them on an individual basis, particularly if that individual is one's self.

Bone's definition of the term "nationalist," formulated during the fifties at a time when few Blacks called themselves nationalist or had given the term their own referents, has an archaic sound today. Contemporary political nationalists not only say to white people, "get off our backs," but get out of our neighborhoods, while the cultural nationalists call for a separate culture whose goals may differ significantly from those of whites. In this context, it is also easy to see that there is little to choose between in Bone's "Negro nationalist" and his "assimilationist." The theoretical concepts which he talks about are probably best labeled Separatist and Integrationist, for as Harold Curse points out, it is the debate between Martin Delany and his spiritual followers in Pan Africanism and Frederick Douglass and his spiritual offspring, the NAACP, which has been the major dialogue among Black people for well over a century.[8]

What Bone actually describes are not, therefore, opposing positions, but, merely, related leitmotifs on a scale similar to the labeling on the "colored-Negro-Black" color wheel. Bone traces his two motifs to a reaction against the prevailing literary stereotypes of Blacks in the second half of the nineteenth century. The motifs, as a subject for dialogue among Black people, go back even further. These two currents of thought were even fused together in an alliance—which was not as tense as Bone's analysis would have one believe—in the narratives of escaped slaves which were such an effective part of the abolitionist campaign prior to the Civil War. Along with revealing the horrors of slavery, an implicit function of the narratives was to prove that, except for the accident of slavery, Black people were just like white people, just as good and just as dull and humdrum.[9]

The principal male figures in most of the novels published prior to 1920 fall on the integrationist side of the scale. Either through an almost total rejection of the Black masses because of their "amoral" ways, their "ungrammatical" speech, their loud "primitive" music and their supposed predilection for the baser things in life, or through an insistence that lower-class Black people, the folk, drop these characteristics and thus earn the right to live in a white society on equal terms, these characters proved that they accepted the white man as a standard of what was good, virtuous and refined.

As heir apparent, Clay differs from his forebears in the fact that he is brought to the realization that no matter how many nigger characteristics he drops, no matter how assimilated he becomes, he is still Black, he is still one of the subject people. He learns, also, that despite all the accouterments of status, the clothing, the education, he can still be commanded to drop back into that old role. But even this knowledge which he is goaded into acquiring is flawed, for he does not learn—or learns too late—that it is impossible to exhibit his newly found learning before the oppressor and live.

It is open to question whether Clay's analysis of Soul is a knowledge which he has consciously lived with for some time and merely verbalizes as a result of Lula's prodding or whether Lula's verbal slashing and jabbing unlock a door which has kept this knowledge hidden away from even his own private eye. One does not, of course, see a light bulb go on in Clay's mind or hear him exclaim, "Aha, color is the issue." One does, however, watch him try valiantly to play Lula's game, to be that which she desires him to be. His explosion, as her thrusts become more painful and her conduct more outrageous, is uncontrollable, at least by him, and once his rage is vented, he turns away from his exposition of the Black heart to give Lula some world-weary advice, as though acknowledging the futility of words as a medium for understanding Blackness or, perhaps, having blown his own game, trying to save Lula from the consequences of hers.

The makings of a hero are there in Clay, the convention breaking, the front, but they never come to fruition. As an Ivy League negro he is by definition an affront to convention, not only because he has stepped out of his assigned place in the social order, but also because he has turned his back upon Black people, or at least the masses of them. An Ivy League or bourgeois negro embraces those social structures or traditions which have oppressed Black people and has, himself, become another kind of stereotype. The narrow shouldered suit, the beard, the aping of Baudelaire are all efforts to forge a new self which has little or nothing to do with Blackness in America. Ironically, all the façades in the world can never hide Clay's skin color which in itself is looked upon as the biggest departure from, and affront to, convention.

Thus Clay's front does not give him that element which is essential to the success of any game, the element of control. He is a victim of his own game; rather than using his front to manipulate others, Clay uses it as a protection not only from white power, that is, the white power structure, but from Black power as well. And, from the moment she enters the coach, Lula does control the situation. *She* picks Clay up. *She* encourages him. And it is she who goads him into revealing things which must have been carefully hidden deep in the most secret places of his heart.

Clay's relationship to the streetman is, at best, tenuous, for while one can imagine a Rinehart holding the same kind of cynical awareness which Clay's façade hides, it is virtually impossible to see him allowing anyone to jockey him into a position where the violence of his own passion creates the fatal self-betrayal of Clay. But Clay denies himself even the simple and logical action of walking away from Lula. He attempts to transmute this rejection of action, this denial of heroism, of identity, into a metaphor ("[*suddenly weary*] Ahhh. Shit. But who needs it? I'd rather be a fool"). Perhaps he would have written a poem—had he survived.

Notes: Chapter 3

1. See, for example, Toni Cade's survey, "Black Theatre," *Black Expression*, pp. 134–142, or *Introduction to New Black Playwrights*, William Couch, ed. (New York: Avon Books, 1970), or the previously cited article by Kgositsile.

2. James Baldwin, "Alas, Poor Richard," *Nobody Knows My Name* (New York: Dell Pub. Co., 1962), p. 191.

3. Charles Gordone, quoted in Phyl Garland, "The Prize Winners," *Ebony* (July 1970), p. 37.

4. LeRoi Jones, *Dutchman and The Slave* (New York: Morrow & Co., 1964), p. 3. Quotations from both plays are from this edition.

5. Lorraine Hansberry, "Me Tink Me Hear Sounds in de Night," *Theatre Arts*, XLIV (Oct. 1960), p. 9.

6. LeRoi Jones, "Jitterbugs," *Black Magic: Poetry 1961–1967* (Indianapolis: Bobbs-Merrill, 1969), p. 92.

7. Bone's definitions do not lend themselves to paraphrasing or interpretation—at least with any reasonable assurance that one has captured what he is trying to convey (as Darwin T. Turner points out in *"The Negro Novel in America:* In Rebuttal," *CLA Journal*, X (Dec. 1966), 122–134). The reader is therefore advised to consult Bone, pp. 25–28.

8. Harold Cruse, *The Crisis of the Negro Intellectual* (New York: Morrow & Co., 1967), p. 6.

9. Jahn, *Neo-African Literature*, pp. 125–130, offers a provocative interpretation of the slave narratives.

CHAPTER FOUR

The Limited Solution of Revolution

(May a lost god damballah, rest or save us
against the murders we intend
against his lost white children
Black dada nihilismus

Amiri Baraka
"Black Dada Nihilismus"
Part II
The Dead Lecturer

| I |

Where *Dutchman* deals in denial, *The Slave* deals in affirmation. Where Clay would refuse to submit to what Baraka seems to feel is the logic and reason of killing in order to put an end to a three-hundred-year-old oppression, Walker Vessels, *The Slave*'s main character, instigates the killing. Clay appears as the epitome of the Integrationist Negro and even when his façade cracks, the perception which he exposes is predictable, given his history over the past three hundred years. His return to passivity at the end of his tirade is a kind of middle-class refusal to act upon the reality which he describes near the end of the play. In *The Slave*, Baraka appears to be presenting Clay's opposite number, the Black Nationalist, a rebel who is heir to the tradition of leadership and revolt forged by Nat Turner, Denmark Vesey and Gabriel Prosser. An artist, however, is adept at the manipulation of fronts and façades. What appears straightforward and real, changes, sometimes imperceptively, to something not quite lifelike, not quite as straightforward as when one first perceived it. Reality becomes a commentary on fantasy and vice versa. And even here in a play which superficially, at least, concerns itself with heroism and rebellion, Baraka mutes the lines between Yea and Nay so that Walker straddles those two currents of Black thought, Integration and Separation, and accepts neither current completely.

Coming from the opposite side of the coin posited by the slave narratives shaped by straitlaced abolitionists, he contends that, except for the accident of economic position, Black people are just like white people, just as selfish and just as ugly. Walker does not love Black people or even freedom; he loves right, reason, sanity—perhaps. He is a revolutionary leader, but he is neither Black rebel nor Black hero. Even as he seeks to end the physical oppression of Black people he—and perhaps his followers, also—remain in psychological bondage to the white man, convinced of the white man's ultimate fitness, because of intelligence, heritage, culture, to rule Black people and the rest of the world. But Walker's conviction that turnabout is indeed fair play is the belief that he acts upon and the battle is joined.

The Black longing for a Messiah is at the center of the

characterization of Walker. The image of intellectual and activist, two strains which have rarely coexisted peacefully in Black life, provides some of the tension in Walker's character. In this fusion of Messiah, intellectual and activist, Baraka creates a character who can stand beside the white anti-heroes of twentieth century America. And the process itself is a commentary on the times and the country.

Embedded deep within the sinews of Black tradition in America is the myth, the hope, really, that some day a Black Messiah will arise from among the people and lead the Black race out of bondage and slavery. This invincible Black man will free his people by any means necessary and lead them into the promised land. The attempted slave rebellions in the first quarter of the nineteenth century, led by Gabriel Prosser and Denmark Vesey, come within the realm of this tradition. Prosser, a slave in Richmond, Virginia, attempted to lead the slaves from the surrounding countryside in revolt. His attempt was foiled by an unexpected and devastating storm and the last minute betrayal by two house servants.[1] Vesey, a free Black man in Charleston, South Carolina, with the help of five lieutenants, roused, coerced and persuaded town and country Blacks into attempting a rebellion. The plan was betrayed by an indiscreet plotter who attempted to recruit the "favorite and confidential slave" of a wealthy planter.[2] The myth has become such an integral part of Black life that one could speak quite casually of the late Martin

Luther King, Jr. as the Negro Moses or of Stokely Carmichael as Super Nigger (the hip, youthful version of
Moses) to a Black audience and the only argument one
would be likely to get was from someone who felt Whitney
Young or Malcolm was his Moses.[3]

The Black war of liberation which forms the background for the play grew out of Walker's planning and
he is commanding general of the Black troops. The atmosphere of the play is pervaded by what one critic has
called a "metaphorical shooting war" between Blacks and
non-Blacks.[4] But the metaphor of *The Slave* is very real
and the sanity which comes to play such an important part
in *Dutchman* is gained, or regained, and the promised
battle is joined.

The play takes place in a city besieged by Black troops,
in the home of Grace and Bradford Easley. Grace, who is
white, is Walker's ex-wife and Easley, who is also white,
is a former friend and colleague of Walker's. Walker has
slipped through the fighting lines to the Easleys' home to
get his children, the offspring of his and Grace's disastrous interracial marriage. Grace and Easley are unwill-
ing to let the children go, and a vast debate ensues, with
Walker and Grace rehashing their marriage and the reasons for its breakup and Grace and Easley castigating
Walker for his part in bringing about the bloody rebellion.
At the end of the play, Easley is dead, killed by Walker;
Grace lies crushed under a fallen beam which was dis-
lodged when a bomb exploded near the house, and

Walker, badly hurt but invincible, slips away. The children are dead or dying. Within the framework of this plot, Baraka sets two tensions to working: the more general and pervading tension caused by the racial war and the personal conflicts of Walker and Grace and Easley. Each character becomes, at times, a spokesman for the viewpoint of his race and a debater in his personal quarrel.

Walker Vessels assumes the cloak of Super Nigger, thus becoming the embodiment of the fusion of those two opposing forces within traditional Black culture, the intellectual and the activist. In his confrontation with Grace and Easley, one sees Walker not as the optimistic, single-minded cinematic hero, but as the disenchanted, almost hopeless, anti-hero out of white literary tradition, who is Super Nigger through necessity rather than choice:

> . . . I have killed for all times any creative impulse I will ever have by the depravity of my murderous philosophies. . . . I am being killed in my head each day and by now have no soul or heart or warmth, even in my long killer fingers. . . . I have no other thing in the universe that I love or trust, but myself . . . all my officers are ignorant motherfuckers who have never read any book in their lives . . . [and] I would rather argue politics, or literature, or boxing, or anything, with you, dear Easley, with you . . .

But Walker has, as he says, "single-handedly, with no other advisor except my own ego, promoted a bloody situation where whites and blacks are killing each other," because,

THE LIMITED SOLUTION OF REVOLUTION

You [Easley] never did anything concrete to avoid what's going on now. Your sick liberal lip service to whatever was the least filth. Your high aesthetic disapproval of the political. Letting the sick ghosts of the thirties strangle whatever chance we [Blacks] had.

Walker's role of Super Nigger is further complicated by his emotional involvement with Grace. The contradictions inherent in Walker's position of a Black revolutionary leader who is emotionally tied to a white woman is illuminated when Grace accuses Walker:

GRACE: You stopped telling me everything!

WALKER: I never stopped telling you I loved you . . .

GRACE: It wasn't enough, Walker. It wasn't enough.

WALKER: God, it should have been.

GRACE: Walker, you were preaching the murder of all white people. Walker, I was, am, white. What do you think was going through my mind every time you were at some rally or meeting whose sole purpose was to bring about the destruction of white people?

WALKER: Oh, goddamn it, Grace, are you so stupid? You were my wife . . . I loved you. You mean because I loved you and was married to you . . . had had children by you, I wasn't supposed to say the things I felt? I was crying out against three hundred years of oppression, not against individuals.

Ironically, Walker shows that he has done the almost impossible thing: He has accepted Grace as a person, free of her history and her race, as a person apart from the hatred, distrust and oppression which has generally characterized relations between Blacks and whites in this country. And Grace refuses to be taken this way. The fact that Walker loved her, loves her, does not obliterate or change the fact that she is white and therefore a part of that three-hundred-year-old relationship. Her position is parallel to that of the post-Stokeley Carmichael Black person who demands to be accepted as *Black*, as a product of an environment different—whether inherently so or through necessity—from its white counterpart. Thus, Baraka implies that a person's color is an important factor in shaping that person's character. And Walker, who does not understand this, is left bewildered and tied to Grace by a knot which is loosened only in death.

Because of this emotional, really humanizing element, the play becomes a minor tragedy in which Walker struggles to reach both the psychological and physical heights of a revolutionary leader but, unable to grapple with his own mind and emotions, falls short of the one even as he reaches the other. Walker is aware that his victory is one-sided and one sees Blacks and non-Blacks together caught up in a horrible dance of mutual annihilation dictated by fate or prophecy or nothing more spectacular than the system under which both live. Hence, one sees Walker move from bitter sarcasm, "Grace Locke Vessels Easley . . . whore of the middle-class," to tenderness, "You were my wife . . . I loved you," to scathing anger, "Believe me, self-righteous little bitch, I want to kill you," in a circle which completes itself only in Grace's death, when Walker walks away from her, from his former friend, from his half-breed children, from all in fact that he has loved in the white world. He ends the play as he began it in the posture of the old field slave from the Prologue, freed now of the oppressive white menace which he sees in Grace and Easley and the system they represent. Walker is still, however, the big buck nigger who must remain Boy until he becomes Uncle, becomes Grandfather; and not all the accouterments of education and refinement can change that. The revolutionary developed out of the field slave and remains slave to the war which will "at best. . . only change the complexion of tyranny," still slave to the idea, first broached in the Prologue, that white folks have had their chance, now the other folks can have theirs.

| II |

". . . now these other folks have their chance. Now they have theirs." Whatever coup the Black forces under Walker are able to pull off, it will be one in which Walker does not share. His world seems to be divided into They (the Blacks), Them (the whites) and Me. While he kills off those things which have held him in fee to the white world and, symbolically, attempts to slay their counterparts within himself, he tries to merge more closely, more securely with the Black world. It is, for him, a hopeless task. Under his leadership, the Blacks have been or will be given "their chance," but he, himself, remains eternally alone, for "their chance" is not his chance.

Walker must take his place beside Clay as another version, admittedly a trifle more radical, of the white hero in blackface, the hero whose values and orientation are white, who really believes that white is right and beautiful. He is reminiscent of the Black minstrels who donned blackface make-up in order to mimic the white, so-called comics who used burnt cork to mock the Blacks who were in turn mocking the pretentious ways of their Southern masters. At the heart of that deception lay ridicule and it is difficult to say who had the last laugh. Walker's black mask continually slips aside to reveal the whiteness which in turn probably hides the fury and self-mocking awareness of Clay. At the heart of Walker's masquerade is a fierce sense of rightness and righteousness that will brook no interference even from the yearnings of his own heart. Whether it is the Blacks, who have at last managed, if not to incorporate that Western sanity and logic into their own lives, at least to make use of it so that they do in fact have their chance; or the whites, fighting to save a civilization which at best is futile, and nuturing all that the arch Black nationalist holds dear, thus making him a victim of his own rhetoric; whether it is either of these two groups who have the last laugh is difficult to answer and is probably beside the point. Certainly, Walker is not laughing. His pain is patent. It is the pain of the chosen, the Lord's anointed who is powerless to abdicate his role.

One senses this pain in Walker's speech for he speaks in sentences studded with elliptical pauses, sentences which teeter on the verge of incoherency but somehow always manage to right themselves in time, sentences which often imply as much as they say in overt statements. And the statements themselves are definite, conclusive and their whole tenor is more often than not at war with the indecisive, elliptical manner in which they are stated.

As the old field slave in the Prologue to the play, Walker addresses the audience on the necessity of appearances:

I am much older than I look . . . or maybe much younger. Whatever I am or seem . . . [*significant pause*] to you, then let that rest. But figure, still, that you might not be right. Figure, still, that you might be lying . . . to save yourself. Or myself's image, which might set you crawling like a thirsty dog, for the meanest of drying streams. The meanest of ideas. [*Gentle mocking laughter*] Yeah. Ideas. Let that settle! Ideas. Where they form. Or whose they finally seem to be. Yours? The others'? Mine? [*Shifts uneasily, pondering the last*] No, no more. Not mine. I served my slow apprenticeship . . . and maybe came up lacking. Maybe. Ha. Who's to say, really? Huh? But figure, still, ideas are still in the world. They need judging. I mean, they don't come in that singular or wild, that whatever they are, just because they're beautiful and brilliant, just because they strike us full in the center of the heart. . . . My God! [*Softer*] My God, just because and even this, believe me, even if, that is, just because they're *right* . . . doesn't mean anything. The very rightness stinks a lotta times. The very rightness. [*Looks down and speaks softer and quicker*] I am an old man. An old man.

He posits another version of reality, his own as opposed to that of his audience, a reality where the "rightness" of an idea (wherever it comes from) does not make it good, or

less "mean." This, of course, is a part of his dilemma as
the leader of the Revolution, that the rightness of the idea
does not make it good or beneficial, especially for himself.
Yet, as leader of the Revolution, his speech, despite
ellipses, leaves nothing out. As he tells Grace:

It took me awhile, but then I finally understood that you did pity
me. And that you were somewhere, going through whatever
mediocre routine you and Easley called your lives . . . pitying
me. I figured that, finally, you weren't really even shocked by
what was happening . . . what had happened. You were so secure
in the knowledge that you were good, and compassionate . . . and
right, that most of all . . . you were certain, my God, so certain
. . . emotionally and intellectually, that you were right, until the
only idea you had about me was to pity me.

By comparison, Easley's speech seems ponderous,
weighted as it is by an effete intellectualism which refuses
action on its own behalf and would deny action to others.

You're filth, boy. Just filth. Can you understand that anything
and everything you do is stupid, filthy, or meaningless! Your
inept formless poetry. Hah. Poetry? A flashy doggerel for in-
ducing all those unfortunate troops of yours to spill their blood
in your behalf. But I guess that's something! Ritual drama, we
used to call it at the university. The poetry of ritual drama.
[*Pulls himself up*] And even that's giving that crap the benefit
of the doubt. Ritual filth would have been the right name for it.

Baraka's rhetoric then, is an instrument, almost a function, of his themes. So that in *Dutchman*, Lula speaks in
images which are often incoherent and chaotic, but whose
words convey their messages almost as much through the

rhythm of the lines which contain them as they do through the meaning of the words. ("All stories are whole stories. All of 'em. Our whole story . . . nothing but change. How could things go on like that forever? Huh? Except I do go on as I do. Apples and long walks with deathless intelligent lovers. But you mix it up. Look out the window all the time. Turning pages. Change, change, change.") Clay's need for precise, concrete information—which will provide him with clues so that he knows what role he is to assume opposite Lula—wars with her rambling imprecision. And it is only when anger has released him from the prison of his buttoned-up suit that he finds his own rhythm, a heady sustained rhythm punctuated by brief staccato half-lines, always driving onward toward a climax which should be action. It is ironic that the action is Lula's and not Clay's.

These two plays are by no means Baraka's definitive works; they merely represent a phase in his development as an artist. Thus, the forlorn beauty of *"The end of man/ is his beauty and silence which proves but a referent to my disorder"*[5] must be contrasted with the celebration of the continuity and togetherness of Black life in "leroy" (. . . *there were black angels/straining above her head, carrying life from our ancestors/and knowledge, and the strong nigger feeling*")[6] The death wish of Clay and Walker must be compared with the will to live which dominates the Black man in *Madheart* and Nasafi and Tanzil in *The Black Mass*. The white man is a secondary concern in

Madheart and *Black Mass* for Baraka's attention is focused on the relationships among Black people and what helps or hinders those relationships from becoming saving forces in Black experience.

In Walker and Clay, Baraka has created two characters with pretensions to heroism. Their pretensions, however, are marred, and fatally so, by their allegiance to the world which destroys them bit by bit as naturally and unconcernedly as it breathes. By fixing them firmly within a tradition which has, at best, sought to find Black solutions within a white framework of thought, the futility of such strivings is proven. Having failed in that context, there is no other alternative except to seek a Black context in which Black people learn to deal with whites, with the Western world, as incidentals which will have increasingly smaller roles to play as Black people attack the task of getting themselves together.

Notes: Chapter 4

1. Harvey Wish, "American Slave Insurrections Before 1861," *Justice Denied*, William M. Chace & Peter Collier, eds. (New York: Harcourt Brace & World, 1970), p. 86.

2. Trial Record of Denmark Vesey, p. 33. It is interesting that this attempt to enlist the aid of a personal servant went against the dictum laid down by Peter, one of Vesey's top lieutenants: "But take care and don't mention it to those waiting men who receive presents of old coats from their masters, or they'll betray us; . . ." p. 17.

THE LIMITED SOLUTION OF REVOLUTION

3. During a memorial for Dr. King in the spring of 1968, the author heard a minister make the usual comparison between Moses and Dr. King. The minister then drew the audience's attention to the fact that while Moses did lead the Hebrew Children to the Promised Land, he, himself, could not go in. It was left to Joshua and the seven priests to lead the battle which won the Promised Land for the Children of Israel. The minister then called for a Joshua to lead the fight which will put Black people in possession of their "Promised Land." Perhaps the concept of a Black Moses is now outmoded.

4. George Dennison, "The Demagogy of LeRoi Jones," *Commentary*, XXXIX (Feb. 1965), p. 66.

5. LeRoi Jones, "The end of man is his beauty," *The Dead Lecturer* (New York: Grove Press, 1964), p. 31.

6. Jones, "leroy," *Black Magic*, p. 217.

III Give Birth to Brightness

How many death songs will we write?

Can we eulogize
sufficiently
the torn
the bleeding
   all
The Dead
         dead flesh
         dead hopes
         dead smiles

Can we count the wasted
hours fill the days to come with
flaking blood/instead of Men?

Neither chants nor wails nor mourning fill
the emptied place obscure the memory nor
heal the heart, what
compensates for
eyes . . .
       gentled at the corners so
   from loving

Mari Evans
"eyes gentled at the corners so"
I Am a Black Woman

CHAPTER FIVE

The Black Musician: The Black Hero as Light Bearer

The Drifters are in the fetid bosom of Manhattan
Rocking the Apollo like an exploding battleship:
The bobbing Black crowd reach long upward
The short-skirted young girls dog in the aisles . . .
    The Drifters are in the big Apple tonight
sing us a song . . . SANG!

.   .   .   .

When I see them strut to the foot lights, faintly
smiling amongst themselves, giving measured "cool" response
to the screaming, the dancing, the reaching, and then looking
into the crowd and darkness, swagger a retreat with that
Elemental sexuality (that has been our only hope for so long)
I love those black bastards with all the heart I dare.

David Henderson
from "Neon Diaspora"
Black Fire

I

The conflict with whites over rights, privileges and status
has played a large and important part in the history of
Black people in this country. This is a commonplace
among historians, sociologists, political scientists and
others who deal with the negro problem. It has been often
and, sometimes, unfortunately, a commonplace among
Black writers. The racial conflict in its many ramifications

135

136

—what racial oppression has done to Blacks and whites, the ways in which Blacks confront and seek to overcome that oppression, etc.—narrows the perspective from which one can view literary characters. For, as a major theme, racial conflict, no matter how radical or startling the situations or solutions, limits even multidimensional characters to roles as either part of the solution or part of the problem. The history of Blacks, and whites, also, is used as a prism which refracts in virtual isolation only a small part of the experience which has gone into making those much entwined histories.

The complexities of the collective Black experience have always had their most valid and moving expression in Black music; music is the chief artifact created out of that experience. Where Black music and Black musicians are used in literature as vehicles for thematic development or as subject matter, however, they are generally touched upon lightly and rarely explored as a theme deserving of individual and primary treatment. Most often, the Black musician and the music he creates are allied with a hedonistic, often raffish, sometimes shiftless way of life which is in conflict with or depicted in contrast to conventional morality and respectability. In novels published during the first three decades of the twentieth century by James Weldon Johnson, Claude McKay and Langston Hughes, the Black music of the period provides a picturesque backdrop, an exotic framework within which the characters attempt to work out their individual destinies.

McKay in *Home to Harlem* (1928) and Hughes in *Not Without Laughter* (1930) make use of the "jazz life"— the rowdy subculture of lower-income Black communities —first characterized by Johnson in *The Autobiography of an Ex-Colored Man* (1912) and popularized by the white negrophile, Carl Van Vechten, in *Nigger Heaven* (1926) as a demi-world where music, dancing, violence and crime rage rampant. Black music becomes, in McKay and Hughes, a symbol of liberation from a stifling respectability and materialistic conventionality which have an odor of decay about them. McKay is content with implying this conflict through the use of the jazz life as a framework for depicting the central characters, Jake and Ray, in *Home to Harlem*.

Unlike McKay's novel, Hughes's *Not Without Laughter* makes a very direct use of music as a symbol of contention, personifying the struggle in the characters of Harriett and Jimboy whose love of secular Black music estranges them from the pious Hagar and the materialistic Tempy, to whom the blues is a godless, vulgar music. Caught between these opposing forces are the young protagonist, Sandy, and his mother, Anjee. Jimboy and Harriett, Sandy's father and his maternal aunt, are laughter and singing; they act out their belief that there is more to life than working for the white man and praising God. This makes them, in the view of Hagar, Sandy's grandmother, and Tempy, another maternal aunt, shiftless and immoral. Hagar's religion is based on forgiveness and turning the other cheek. Heaven is for her the ultimate happiness; she looks for neither happiness nor fun in the earthly world. The gaiety and desire to be near bright lights and laughter, which is so much a part of the nature of her youngest daughter, Harriett, finds no echoing response in her. For Tempy, religion is a means of expressing her rising status in the world; "refinement" in deportment, dress and worship is her way of signaling her economic distance from her rural, poverty-stricken origins. Blues and ragtime are not so much immoral as niggerish, manifestations of the very characteristics which Tempy thinks are uncultured and ignorant and from which, in her upward climb, she disassociates herself. Both Hagar and Tempy believe that only in work can Black people find salvation; for Hagar, salvation is spiritual, for Tempy it is material.

Anjee, Hagar's second daughter, is, in nature, somewhat like her mother. She is pious and generous, but more phlegmatic and less far seeing. She yearns toward the gaiety and laughter of her husband, is in fact fascinated by them, and can no more stop loving Jimboy than she can willingly stop breathing. Despite the fact that, after almost ten years of being left behind as Jimboy wanders from town to town and job to job, she does pack up and join him, her own nature remains unchanged by her contact with the flame that is Jimboy. She is, if anything, duller, more plodding at the novel's end than at its beginning.

Sandy is influenced by the opposing forces and he

achieves a synthesis which allows him to take the best from the warring life styles. Despite the hardships involved, he decides to return to school. Hughes, however, makes it clear that it is not a step in the status-seeking climb toward white respectability which motivates Sandy's choice:

'. . . I'm going back to my classes in September. . . . I'm through with elevators.'

Jimboy! Jimboy! Like Jimboy! something inside him warned, quitting work with no money, uncaring.

'Not like Jimboy,' Sandy countered against himself. 'Not like my father, always wanting to go somewhere. I'd get as tired of traveling all the time as I do of running this elevator up and down day after day. . . . I'm more like Harriett—not wanting to be a servant at the mercies of white people forever. . . . I want to do something for myself, by myself. . . . Free. . . . I want a house to live in, too, when I'm older—like Tempy and Mr. Sile's. . . . But I wouldn't want to be like Tempy's friends—or her husband, dull and colorless, putting all his money away in a white bank, ashamed of colored people.'

Characteristically, Hughes amplifies Sandy's decision through a further use of the symbol of Black music.

Clowns! Jazzers! Band of dancers! . . . But was that why Negroes were poor, because they were dancers, jazzers, clowns? . . . The other way round would be better: dancers because of their poverty; singers because they suffered; laughing all the time because they must forget. . . . It's more like that, thought Sandy.

A band of dancers. . . . Black dancers—captured in a white world. . . . Dancers of the spirit, too. Each Black dreamer a captured dancer of the spirit.[1]

Music is refuge, release, expression. But Hughes and Mc-
Kay make no attempt to go beyond the relatively simple
equation that Black music is Black escape from the dead-
ening restraints of white civilization. They make no
further attempt to explore the themes presented by the
Black musician or his music. In this, they depart from the
path first tentatively explored in Johnson's novel. For
Johnson, in the fictional *Autobiography of an Ex-Colored
Man*, depicts the losing battle of a half-white musician
turned businessman who struggles to affirm himself in the
heritage and culture of his mother's people. His hope of
creating a place for Black music among serious Western
classical music is not enough to compensate for his own
lack of strength. The nameless central character finally
trades his Black musical heritage with its attendant pain,
suffering and humiliation for the less terrifying but more
profitable life of a white businessman. For the character,
this retreat into passing for white is a defeat which he
recognizes as his own willingness to accept the non-threat-
ening aspects of his heritage—Black music and the supposed Black exoticism—and his lack of the psychological
and physical strength to withstand the terrifying forms
which racism often takes, even though these forms are also
a part of the Black heritage. Music is a metaphor and
symbol standing in both its secular and sacred forms not
only for the immediate Black experience as in McKay and
Hughes, but for history and heritage and the acceptance
of one's self in a positive and regenerating relationship

to that heritage. The protagonist in attempting to garner serious attention and respect for the music seeks to add another dimension to the image of a rude boisterous music created by a poverty-stricken, ignorant people.

It is again tempting to try to fit these novels completely within the Western literary tradition of the literature of roguery—the picaresque. Certainly there are elements which might be termed picaresque in all three novels: the episodic plots, the characters of uncertain or nameless origins from the lowest strata of society, the alienation from the larger society which is inherent in their skin color and the chaotic nature of the society, symbolized in the supposed chaos of the music's structure and more accurately suggested by the fact that the music is itself a way of structuring, ordering or relieving the pressures of society's chaos. But to confine the Black musician to the picaresque mode as a means of interpretation is to obscure an essential quality of his image. The Black musician, the jazz, blues or gospel artist, in crystallizing and synthesizing his own experience and that of his listeners, exemplifies unity and community rather than the alienation and isolation of the picaro.

The character of the Black musician must be viewed as a figure in the modern Black parallel to the picaresque existence, street life—the jazz life in the novels of Hughes, McKay and Johnson. Even here, in a world pervaded by various types of hustlers and con men, the Black musician stands in a unique light. Although he, like the other figures in the street life, deals in dreams, he is not a hustler for he also deals in love. When he touches, both in technique and emotion, the roots of his own past and the past of his Black listeners, putting them all in touch with the heart's ache and the heart's ease of that group experience, he makes a black light to shine within himself and within them. And it is that light, transitory as it is, which binds them all together.

But what happens in the dance hall, night club, church sanctuary or theatre stage seldom finds a parallel in the outside world. The power and cathartic effect which he has been able to exercise through the use of his instrument or his voice rarely holds sway there. Off the bandstand or outside the church, the musician becomes just another Black who can be messed over, messed with and messed up just like anybody else—perhaps more so. For the sensitivity to emotions, situations and their nuances, which allows him to transmute his life experience into music, also makes him more vulnerable to the more painful and abrasive aspects of that experience. And when he has been rubbed so raw that pain and joy can no longer be translated or transmuted into art, he is very much in trouble.

The Black musician in trouble is the figure which most often appears in Black literature. This growing body of work extends the theme first broached in the novels of Johnson and McKay, the poetry of Sterling Brown and the poetry and fiction of Langston Hughes. In their tentative explorations of the relationship between Black life and Black music—the trials and joys of being Black in the white man's world—they lay the foundation for the portrayal of the musician who brings together the sublime and beautiful, the complex and brutal pieces of his experience in his music and finally is torn apart himself by the very complexity and brutality which he has helped to ameliorate. Clay, the protagonist in *Dutchman*, gives a beautiful summation of this theme when he tells his white antagonist Lula: "If Bessie Smith had killed some white people, she wouldn't have needed that music. She could have talked very straight and plain about the world. No metaphors. No grunts. No wiggles in the dark of her soul. Just straight two and two are four. Money. Power. Luxury. Like that."[2]

There is truth in this view, a limited truth. That pain plays a large part in Black music is evident in the lyrics of the blues, the spirituals, the gospels, in the raw harshness which has been such an important aspect in the development of jazz. Yet, there is the beautiful lyricism of Charlie Parker and John Coltrane which also expresses triumph and transcendence, the sly humor and laughing confidence, the will to make it on through, to work it on out which are also expressed in blues, gospels and spirituals. The former view is predicated upon two assumptions: the first that had the Emancipation Proclamation and the amendments which broadened its effects and meaning been followed in spirit and letter, that ragtime, blues and jazz would never have been created. It sees Black music primarily as a response to an outside stimulus rather than to an inner drive which would have found expression no matter what the circumstance. The second assumption is perhaps more serious for it strikes at the very basis of Black music, its communal roots. It assumes that the music is more an affirmation of self than an affirmation of self in relation to group, that the musician creates an interior monologue rather than a dialogue between and about himself and the group and their past and present. Thus to concur wholeheartedly in Clay's solution is to overlook the fact that killing white people will not necessarily make a Black person love himself or others. A part of the lesson of Clay and Walker is that whatever the relationship between Blacks and whites, Black people must still deal with each other and themselves.

Recognizing that Black life is, in large measure, Black music, several writers have used the musician as a symbol of the centuries of culture and tradition which stand behind American Blacks. The musician, then, becomes a heightened example of what can and does happen to Black people, and his salvation perhaps points the way to theirs. Unlike the other figures in the Life, the musician does not need to be told that his source is the group, the Black context; his music already provides that model. In being recalled to the group, his need is for a spiritual or physical bridge to span the gulf between his music and his life.

In Blacksnake Brown, Jane Phillips (*Mojo Hand*, 1965) creates a shamanesque figure who initiates the heroine into the deeper meanings of Black life and experi-

ence. The crude vulgar musician, Richie, depicted in
Night Song (Williams, 1962) is akin to the tortured musical genius described by Clay, as is Ludlow Washington,
the blind saxophonist in William Melvin Kelley's *A Drop
of Patience* (1965). The latter two are driven in part by a
self-hatred which wars with their love of music, that is,
their love of Blackness. Richie's personal dilemma is
finally resolved in death, a death which is largely predicated upon his own self-destructive traits. Ludlow returns
to the group experience which produced him, realizing at
the novel's end that the pursuit of fame as a jazz artist in
night clubs and concert halls is unimportant compared to
the need of Black people for Black musicians who will
speak to them and for them in the forums of their own
communities. It is also his need, for in order to be at peace
with himself he has to be with his own people.

| II |

The musician in the works of James Baldwin is more than
a metaphor; he is the embodiment of alienation and estrangement, which the figure of the artist becomes in much
of twentieth century literature. Most of his characters have
at the center of their portrayal an isolation from the society, the culture, even each other. They are also commen-
taries upon the brutal, emasculating, feared—and fearing
—land from which they are so estranged. The musician is
also for Baldwin an archetypal figure whose referent is

Black lives, Black experiences and Black deaths. He is the hope of making it in America and the bitter mockery of never making it well enough to escape the danger of being Black, the living symbol of alienation from the past and hence from self and the rhythmical link with the mysterious ancestral past. That past and its pain and the transcendence of pain is always an implicit part of the musician's characterization in Baldwin. Music is the medium through which the musician achieves enough understanding and strength to deal with the past and present hurt.

The short story, "Sonny's Blues," sketches this kind of relationship between the individual and his personal and group history. Sonny is a jazz pianist who has recently returned from a drug cure. The story is set in New York, Harlem, and seems at first glance merely another well-written story about a young Black man trying to become himself, to attain his majority and retain his humanity amid all the traps which have been set to prevent just that. But the simplicity of the tale is only surface deep; in a rising crescendo of thematic complexity, the present struggle is refracted through the age-old pain, the age-old life force. The story is narrated by Sonny's older brother who has found it difficult to understand what music means to Sonny. Sonny's desire to be a jazz musician, which his brother associates with the "good-time" life, has created a schism between himself and his more orthodox brother. And because the brother cannot understand what lies be-

tween himself and Sonny, he cannot forgive Sonny for
Sonny's own pain, which he, for all his seniority, is powerless to ease, or for the pain which their ruptured relationship has caused him. The closing pages of the story are a
description of the brother's reaction as he listens to Sonny
play for the first time.

All I know about music is that not many people ever really hear
it. And even then, on the rare occasions when something opens
within, and the music enters, what we mainly hear, or hear cor-
roborated, are personal, private, vanishing evocations. But the
man who creates the music is hearing something else, is dealing
with the roar rising from the void and imposing order on it as
it hits the air. What is evoked in him, then, is of another order,
more terrible because it has no words, and triumphant, too, for
that same reason. And his triumph, when he triumphs, is ours.
I just watched Sonny's face. His face was troubled, he was working hard, but he wasn't with it.

The attempt to once again make it through music brings
no instant transformation. Sonny is approaching the center of his life and he cannot know what he will find there.
But he understands that if he is to live, he must deal with
that dread, that terror, chance the terrifying in order to
triumph.

And I had the feeling that, in a way, everyone on the bandstand
was waiting for him, both waiting for him and pushing him
along. But as I began to watch Creole, I realized that it was
Creole who held them all back. He had them on a short rein. Up
there, keeping the beat with his whole body, wailing on the
fiddle, with his eyes half closed, he was listening to everything,
but he was listening to Sonny. He was having a dialogue with

Sonny. He wanted Sonny to leave the shoreline and strike out for the deep water. He was Sonny's witness that deep water and drowning were not the same thing—he had been there, and he knew. And he wanted Sonny to know. He was waiting for Sonny to do the things on the keys which would let Creole know that Sonny was in the water.

The musical group, Ellison's "marvel of social organization,"[3] is the catalyst which makes it possible for Sonny to begin to see himself through the music, to play out his own pain through the expression of it.

And Sonny hadn't been near a piano for over a year. And he wasn't on much better terms with his life, not the life that stretched before him now. . . . And the face I saw on Sonny I'd never seen before. Everything had been burned out of it, and, at the same time, things usually hidden were being burned in, by the fire and fury of the battle which was occurring in him up there.

Yet, watching Creole's face as they neared the end of the first set, I had the feeling that something had happened, something I hadn't heard. . . . Creole started into something else, it was almost sardonic, it was *Am I Blue*. And, as though he commanded, Sonny began to play. Something began to happen. And Creole let out the reins. The dry, low, black man said something awful on the drums. Creole answered, and the drums talked back. Then the horn insisted, sweet and high, slightly detached perhaps, and Creole listened, commenting now and then, dry, and driving, beautiful and calm and old. Then they all came together again, and Sonny was part of the family again. I could tell this from his face. He seemed to have found, right there beneath his fingers, a damn brand-new piano. It seemed that he couldn't get over it. Then, for awhile, just being happy with Sonny, they seemed to be agreeing with him that brand-new pianos certainly were a gas.

Sonny's music and his life become one and he is fused with the musical group in a relationship which sustains one because it sustains all. And finally, through the music, Sonny's brother begins to understand not so much Sonny, as himself, *his* past, *his* history, *his* traditions and that part of himself which he has in common with Sonny and the long line of people who have gone before them.

Then Creole stepped forward to remind them that what they were playing was the blues. He hit something in all of them, he hit something in me, myself, and the music tightened and deepened, apprehension began to beat the air. Creole began to tell us what the blues were all about. They were not about anything very new. He and his boys up there were keeping it new, at the risk of ruin, destruction, madness, and death, in order to find new ways to make us listen. For, while the tale of how we suffer, and how we are delighted, and how we may triumph is never new, it always must be heard. There isn't any other tale to tell, it's the only light we've got in all this darkness.

And this tale, according to that face, that body, those strong hands on those strings, has another aspect in every country, and a new depth in every generation. Listen, Creole seemed to be saying, listen. Now these are Sonny's blues. He made the little black man on the drums know it, and the bright, brown man on the horn. Creole wasn't trying any longer to get Sonny in the water. He was wishing him Godspeed. Then he stepped back, very slowly, filling the air with the immense suggestion that Sonny speak for himself.

Then they all gathered around Sonny, and Sonny played. Every now and again one of them seemed to say, amen. Sonny's fingers filled the air with life, his life. But that life contained so many others. And Sonny went all the way back, he really began with the spare, flat statement of the opening phrase of the song. Then he began to make it his. It was very beautiful because it wasn't hurried and it was no longer a lament. I seemed to hear with what burning he had made it his, with what burning we had yet to make it ours, how we could cease lamenting. Freedom lurked around us and I understood, at last, that he could help us to be free if we would listen, that he would never be free until we did. Yet, there was no battle in his face now. I heard what he had gone through, and would continue to go through until he came to rest in earth. He had made it his: that long line, of which we knew only Mama and Daddy. And he was giving it back, as everything must be given back, so that, passing through death, it can live forever.[4]

It is this then, this intense, almost excruciating, but always sustaining relationship among musicians and between them and their audiences which the musician is meant to evoke. The emphasis is gradually transformed from pain to survival to life. All are linked together by invisible webs, indestructible bonds of tradition and history, and this heritage, once revealed, becomes the necessary regenerative power which makes life possible. One senses this in Rufus, the drummer and central character in the first Book of *Another Country*, for as Baldwin says in describing the last set of Rufus's last gig:

... during the last set, [Rufus] came doubly alive because the saxophone player, who had been way out all night, took off on a terrific solo.

. . . .

The men on the stand stayed with him, cool and at a little distance, adding and questioning and corroborating, holding it down as well as they could with an ironical self-mockery, but each man knew that the boy was blowing for every one of them [5]

But this relationship is subverted and eventually destroyed by Rufus's involvement with a Southern white woman, Leona, a poor, plain girl-woman whom Baldwin seems to posit as one part of the reality behind the myth of sacred Southern white womanhood. But in grappling with her, Rufus is hedged about by the brutality of the past and his own slender personal resources. The integration of past and present is always on the level of pain and never that of life. The strength which made it possible for his ancestors to endure and to survive that pain is buried somewhere within Rufus, in a place which he does not even realize exists. He becomes more entangled with Leona, wallowing in an ancient source of pain, but never calls upon his family, or his music, the symbols of life, the talismen against death which might have been his salvation—and Leona's. He attempts to use sex as a weapon against her in the same way in which white society has used sex as a weapon against him. The "terrible muscle" and the "violent deep," the male and female sexual organs in Baldwin's works, are always, when used as weapons, self-destructive. Leona is driven insane by Rufus's brutal treatment of her. Rufus, weighted down with guilt and the pain of both past and present, commits suicide.

Baldwin attempts to establish a contrasting structure between this relationship and the relationship which develops between Vivaldo, the white boy who had been his best friend, and Ida, his beloved younger sister. Rufus and Leona end their lives in despair and death, while Vivaldo and Ida, drawn together at first by the love they both had for Rufus, finally achieve an uneasy peace with each other. It is a peace, which, though hard won and perhaps easily lost, is based on a deeper understanding of themselves and each other and their relationship. Rufus returns to the past and cannot find his way out again. But Vivaldo, in his relationship with Ida, tries to move into the future, to break the mold of degradation and humiliation which has usually characterized the relationship of white men with Black women.

Rufus's struggle informs the other two Books in the novel, and the characters are defined and distinguished through their relationship to him. The strength of the first Book, however, its technical and thematic brilliance, finds only dim echoes in these later portions and it is the agony of Rufus as he seeks to reconcile the past hate with the present love and his tragic failure which dominates the novel.

In *Blues for Mister Charlie,* the outline sketched in "Sonny's Blues" becomes a tumultuous and vivid portrayal of that history and tradition which has made Black experience Black life. Richard has lost touch with the group, abused himself and his tradition and fallen back on drugs as a means of making it through the world. Because of his drug thing, he is out of step, out of time and the play, in part, deals with Richard's attempt to get back in step, to find that lost group rhythm.

| III |

The coming together of the group and the individual, of Richard and the Black chorus, in *Blues for Mister Charlie* is sparked by Juanita, the young woman whom he comes to love and who loves him. But the union takes place on a level which seems to have been too subtle for most reviewers to note. Typical of these analyses is Edward Margolies' comment that Richard is "highly neurotic, obstreperous, and disagreeable." Margolies sees Richard's only claim to heroism, "if," as he carefully modifies it, "it can be called that," as Richard's ability to articulate all the venom and bitterness he feels toward whites. It is an act of courage, but there is little else about him that is admirable."[6] Margolies has perhaps been overcome by Baldwin's scathing indictment of white people. While one would certainly not want to stop Baldwin from indicting all the white people he wants, one of the central concerns of the play, the growth of Richard, is likely to be overlooked as Black audiences applaud, Right on! and white audiences squirm and cry, Not so! The indictment of racism is merely a backdrop for the character of Richard and all he represents as musician and Black man.

The action of *Blues for Mister Charlie* centers around the return of Richard to his home in a small Southern town. Richard runs afoul of one of the town's most notorious racists, who murders him. The murderer, Lyle Britten, is tried by an all-white jury and acquitted. The atmosphere of the play is dominated, in part, by a white chorus whose movements are the stylized motions of not very lifelike dolls. The mechanical quality is intentional and the motions and emotions of the white town rise to an almost sexual climax during the third act courtroom scenes where the chorus attempts to castrate and/or impale Black witnesses on the spikes of their own sexual fears. Lyle, the murderer, Jo, his wife, and Parnell, the liberal, would-be friend of white and Black stand out against the chorus, not because they are different, but because they are heightened, more humanized forms of the fears and repressions, hopes, loves and lusts of the whitetown chorus.

On the other side of the street, literally, is the Black chorus, seemingly drawn in different directions but united in the need to win free of the yoke of oppression whose reins are held by whitetown. There is fury and rage in them, but also tenderness and a painful driving energy which struggles for release in Richard, Meridian, his father, and Juanita. The third act brings the Blacktown chorus no release, no climax, for though their presence has helped the Black witnesses resist the repeated attempts to humiliate and degrade them, the courtroom verdict is no more than they expected. It merely confirms the necessity of finding a release for the fury which Richard's death has intensified.

Richard is a musician, a singer, and the first time he is evoked in the play as a person it is through his songs.

THE BLACK HERO AS LIGHT BEARER

MOTHER HENRY: You remember that song [Richard] used to like so much?

MERIDIAN: I sing because I'm happy.

JUANITA: I sing because I'm free.

PETE: For his eye is on the sparrow—

LORENZO: And I know he watches—me.

JUANITA: There was another song he liked—a song about a prison and the light from a train that shone on the prisoners every night at midnight. I can hear him now: Lord, you wake up in the morning. You hear the ding-dong ring—

MOTHER HENRY: He had a beautiful voice.

LORENZO: Well, he was pretty tough up there in New York—til he got busted.

.   .   .   .

JUANITA: You go a-marching to the table, you see the same old thing—

JIMMY: All I'm going to tell you: knife, a fork, and a pan—

PETE: And if you say a thing about it—

LORENZO: You are in trouble with the man.[7]

But it is not so much the "man" whom Richard is in trouble with, as with himself. The audience first sees him standing in his room singing, so that one is made aware from the start of the frantic power and the glory, too, of Richard the artist:

We discover Richard, standing in his room, singing. This number is meant to make vivid the Richard who was much loved on the Apollo Theatre stage in Harlem, the Richard who was a rising New York star.

Richard left the South during his adolescence compelled by the outside force of his father's need to save him from growing up in the town which, perhaps literally, had killed Richard's mother and impelled by his own inner sense of his father's powerlessness before the white world. His father could not even protect his mother and Richard sees himself in his father's lack of power. But Richard finds in the ambiguities of the North—ambiguities which are no more than masks for the same pathological race attitudes from which he fled—no solace, no peace.

... [Aunt Edna] said it wasn't as tight for a black man up there as it is down here. Well, that's a crock, Grandmama, believe me when I tell you. At first I thought it was true, hell, I was just a green country boy and they ain't got no signs up, dig, saying you can't go here or you can't go there. No, you got to find that out all by your lonesome. But—for awhile—I thought everything was swinging . . .

In Richard's first scenes, his knowledge of his own weakness, and the weakness of Black men, is patent. He acknowledges his own helplessness and the Black man's inability to protect his woman, and then, immediately, partly to bolster his own ego, partly to make up in sexuality what he lacks in power, he speaks of his conquest of white women:

[White men are] jive mothers. They can rape our women and we can't do nothing. But if we touch one of their dried-up, pale-assed women, we get our nuts cut off. You remember that chick I was telling you about earlier, lives in Greenwich Village in New York? . . . She's *white*, man. I got a whole *gang* of white chicks in New York. That's *right*. And they can't get enough of what little Richard's got—and I give it to them, too, baby, believe me. You say black people ain't got no dignity? Man, you ought to watch a white woman when she wants you to give her a little bit. They will do anything, baby *any*thing!

Juanita sees through this device, sees the sadness behind his bravado, sees that Richard's use of white women is finally no more than an outlet for the thwarted rage he feels for white society and, most particularly, for white men. For Richard, crippled by his sense of weakness, has to parade his sexuality because he feels it is the one thing he has left which makes him a man. And when even this pretended power loses its effectiveness, he turns to drugs.

See, I couldn't stand these chicks I was making it with, and I was working real hard at my music, and, man, I was lonely. You come off a gig, you be tired, and you'd already taken as much shit as you could stand from the managers and the people in the room you were working and you'd be off to make some down scene with some pasty white-faced bitch. And so you'd make the scene and somehow you'd wake up in the morning and the chick would be beside you, alive and well, and dying to make the scene again and somehow you'd managed not to strangle her, you hadn't beaten her to death. Like you wanted to. And you get out of there and you carry this pain around inside all day and all night long. No way to beat it—no *way*. No matter how you turned, no matter what you did—no *way*. But when I started getting high, I was cool, and it didn't bother me. And I wasn't lonely then, it was all right. And the chicks—I could handle them, they couldn't reach me. And I didn't know I was hooked—until I was *hooked*.

But even cured of drugs he must still brag of his potency before Juanita, before Pete, before Lyle Britten and it is only when he realizes that another beautiful person sees his beauty and will respond to it and care for him, that he no longer needs to brag, no longer needs to issue challenges. As he says:

> . . . I'm beginning to understand my life—for the first time. I can look back and it doesn't hurt me like it used to. . . . I been in pain and darkness all my life. All my life. And this is the first time in my life I've ever felt—maybe it isn't all like that. Maybe there's more to it than that.

He understands his father and something of what his father has gone through, has had to live. And he is now able to tuck his past, and that of his father's and his father's father, around him like an old but loved cloak, for remembering brings not only pain but strength and selfhood.

His newly found selfhood, however, is a challenge in itself, for it means that others must now relate to him in a new way. Even Lyle Britten's dogged need to prove his masculinity at Richard's expense does not shake Richard's newly defined self. Thus it is that the wild challenge, the almost hysterical taunting which characterized his first confrontation with Lyle, is absent from his death scene. Here, Richard wants only to be left alone, to disengage himself from the society which had made it necessary for him to use white women and drugs in order to feel that he existed. There is a quiet dignity in his

> Why don't you go home [Lyle]? And let me go home? Do we need all this shit? Can't we live without it? . . . [I'm] tired of all this fighting. What are you trying to prove? What am I

trying to prove? . . . I'm hip [that] you been trying to give me a break for a great, long time. But there's only one break I want. And you won't give me that . . . For you to go home. And let me go home. I got things to do. I got—lots of things to do! . . . Can't we walk? Let me walk, white man! Let me walk! . . . [Our business is] settled. You a man and I'm a man. Let's walk.

But Lyle, the white man, refuses to admit that he has even heard what is a request from one man to another. And Richard is forced to school him, to speak to Lyle as one would to a young and not very much loved child. Speaking in the collective voice of Black men, he lays bare the phoniness, the fakery, at the root of Lyle's masculinity and dignity.

You sick mother! Why can't you leave me alone? White man! I don't want nothing from you. You ain't got nothing to give me. You can't eat because none of your sad-assed chicks can cook. You can't talk because won't nobody talk to you. You can't dance because you've got nobody to dance with—don't you know I've watched you all my life? *All my life!* And *I* know your women, don't you think I don't—better than you!

(*Lyle shoots, once.*)

Why have you spent so much time trying to kill me? Why you always trying to cut off *my* cock? You worried about it? Why?

(*Lyle shoots again.*)

Okay. Okay. Okay. Keep your old lady home, you hear? Don't let her near no nigger. She might get to like it, too. Wow!

(*Richard falls* [with the names of his father, mother and Juanita on his lips].)

Sex is a metaphor for power but the power which it symbolizes is a sham, a façade behind which lurks the weakness of those—both white and Black—who would use it
as an instrument of subjugation or oppression. Baldwin
implies that this is the great tragedy of white people, that
sex is for them only a means of claiming, of dominating
others, that there is all take and very little give in their
relationships. There is, as Juanita remarks of Parnell, no
flesh they can really touch. Or, it is like Parnell's play on
words, "peace" and "piece" in the third act. Peace is
union with a citadel, a Jo Britten, to whom the mind is
a citadel from which all thoughts of sexuality must be
chased. She thinks, instead, of possessions and material
things. Marriage becomes nothing more than an escape
from the fear of having "to spend the rest of [her] life
serving coffee to strangers in church basements." Peace
is something divorced from heat or warmth and it is indeed a very sobering thought, while "piece" is "poontang," the debased but life-giving fire of a Black woman.
In acquiring, in mastering, both the "peace" and the
"piece" the white man proves anew, with his penis, now,
instead of his whip or his money or his law, his superiority over the Black man. Lyle, the poor white man, puts
the two together and builds his life on this and when
Richard tells him by his actions that both his citadel and
his poontang are mere imitations of the reality which
he, Richard, possesses, Lyle kills him, for Richard has
threatened his very life.

Parnell, the rich liberal, is Lyle's best friend, his other, thinking half. He sees quite clearly the willful self-delusions at the basis of Lyle's life and his own:

Christ, how weary I am of this dull calisthenic called love—with no love in it! . . . Using her [his white girl friend] as an anchor —to hold me here, in this house, this bed—so I won't find myself on the other side of town, ruining my reputation.

He is drawn to the other side of town by its vitality, its regenerative strength. But the feeling that there must be something depraved, unclean about life in the midst of so much squalor and tragedy persists:

All your life you've been made sick, stunned, dizzy, oh, Lord! driven half mad by blackness. Blackness in front of your eyes. Boys and girls, men and women—you've bowed down in front of them all! And then hated yourself. Hated yourself for debasing yourself? Out with it Parnell! The nigger-lover! Black boys and girls! I've wanted my hands full of them, wanted to drown them, laughing and dancing and making love—making love— wow!—and be transformed, formed, liberated out of this grey-white envelope.

And finally he is thrown back upon the aridness, the paucity of soul force in his own life:

I give nothing! How dare she say that! My girl, if you knew what I've given! Ah. Come off it, Parnell. To *whom* have you given?

And just as clearly, Richard moves beyond Parnell's vision, can, in fact, no longer be touched by it. He comes full circle and the unity of experience which was sundered by his mother's death is renewed by Juanita's life and

love. The idea of a circular movement is reinforced on a
more obvious level by the fact that Richard and Juanita
were childhood friends, almost sweethearts, and had Richard remained in their hometown, they, as he remarks to
Meridian, would probably have been married and have
a couple of kids.

As it is, the two of them bring another kind of awareness to their renewed relationship. Richard has been down
the road a little and Juanita has remained fecund, waiting,
unconsciously, for the touch which is Richard's. She questions him about his "illness" not out of curiosity but out
of concern:

JUANITA: . . . what was the matter with you, Richard, what
were you sick with?
RICHARD: It wasn't serious. And I'm better now.
JUANITA: Well, no, that's just it. You're not really better.
RICHARD: How do you mean?
JUANITA: I watch you—
RICHARD: *Why* do you watch me?
JUANITA: I care about you.
RICHARD: You care about me! I thought you could hold your
liquor better than that, girl.
JUANITA: It's not liquor. Don't you believe that anyone can
care about you?
RICHARD: Care about me! Do you know how many times
chicks have told me that? That they *cared* about me?
JUANITA: Well. This isn't one of those times.

And Richard, sensing that this may not be "one of those
times," returns to the idea, testing it, "So you care about

me, do you? Ain't that a bitch?" for he finds it hard to believe that someone can.

In a richly evocative scene, Juanita broaches the idea of their going through the world together:

JUANITA: . . . I won't let you go anywhere without me.

RICHARD: You *still* determined to break your neck.

JUANITA: Well, it's a neck-breaking time. I wouldn't like to appear to be above the battle.

RICHARD: Do you have any idea of what you might be letting yourself in for?

JUANITA: No. But you said you were lonely. And I'm lonely, too.

At exactly what point Richard begins to believe that Juanita can and does care about him is not important. What is important is that he does come to believe and it is this belief which reinforces his sense of identity, and his "I know I can do it. I know I can do it" refers not so much to the knowledge that he can ask Juanita to marry him, that he can take her away with him, as it does to the knowledge that he can take care of her and protect her as his father had not been able to care for or protect his mother.

Richard is linked to the blacktown chorus by the color of his skin and through the common roots of their history and experience. Through his relationship with Juanita, the link, despite his death, remains concrete and alive, for if loving Juanita makes a man of Richard, he makes a woman of her. As she explains to Pete, the Black man who wants to take Richard's place in her life:

GIVE BIRTH TO BRIGHTNESS

When Richard came, he—*hit*—me in some place where I'd never been touched before. I don't mean—just physically. He took all my attention—the deepest attention, maybe, that one person can give another. He needed me and he made a difference for me in this terrible world—do you see what I mean? And—it's funny—when I was with him, I didn't think of the future, I didn't dare. I didn't know if I could be strong enough to give him what he needed for as long as he would need it. It only lasted four or five days, Pete—four or five days, like a storm, like lightning! And what I saw during that storm I'll always see. Before that—I thought I knew who I was. But now I know that there are more things in me than I'll ever understand—

Or again, as she tells Parnell before Lyle Britten's trial, "One day. I'll recover [from the pain of Richard's death]. I'm sure that I'll recover. And I'll see the world again—the marvelous world. And I'll have learned from Richard —how to love." This is spoken in the comparative calm after the shock and pain of Richard's death have eased somewhat. But even in the wildness of grief, enough of Richard's grace—for there is no other word to describe the power and beauty which characterize Richard in those last moments of his life—clings to Juanita so that she can acknowledge that the long lines of Black people brought to fruition in her and in Richard does not stop in her body or end in Richard's death.

How [Richard] clung [to me], how he struggled—life and death! Life and death! Why did it all seem like tears? That he came to me, clung to me, plunged into me, sobbing, howling, bleeding, somewhere inside his chest, his belly, and it all came out, came pouring out, like tears! My God . . . Richard! Why couldn't I have held you closer? Held you, held you, borne you, given you life again? Have made you be born again! Oh, Richard. . . . I hope I'm pregnant. I *hope* I am! One more illegitimate black baby—that's right, you jive mothers! And I'm going to raise my baby to be a man. A *man*, you dig? Oh, let me be pregnant, let me be pregnant, don't let it all be gone! . . . A man. Oh, my God, there are no more. For me. Did this happen to Mama sometime? Did she have a man sometime who vanished like smoke? And left her to get through this world as best she could? Is that why she married my father? . . . Is this how we all get to be mothers—so soon? of helpless men—because all the other men perish? . . . I will end up taking care of some man, some day. Help me do it with love. Pete. Meridian, Parnell. We have been the mothers for them all. It must be dreadful to be Parnell. There is no flesh he can touch. All of it is bloody.

If there is no compassion, no sympathy for Parnell in this brief acknowledgement, there is the awareness that Parnell's barrenness and, perhaps, that of whites has somehow touched and stained Black people. The focus here, however, has changed from castigating those who have touched them, as Richard does earlier in the play— to how they may free themselves from the barrenness of those touches. Thus, when Juanita acquiesces to Parnell's request to accompany her and the blacktown chorus to the church at the end of the play, it is out of a sense of her own hard-won selfhood and womanhood and the knowledge that easing her own pain does not necessarily mean causing pain to others. Her action does not absolve him of his complicity in Lyle's acquittal, nor is it meant to; rather, it removes Parnell to the outer fringe of her life as she joins with blacktown in the problem of getting on with Black life.

Richard sees the group tradition as weak, powerless. He seeks to define himself in opposition to it as powerful, a conqueror. It is only when he discovers that pain endured in seeming docility and passivity does not need to be a source of humiliation and continuing shame, that he can draw on the life-giving force represented by that experience. He learns that he need not fear pain, for he and his people have been there before; having made it through once, they can make it through again.

Notes: Chapter 5

1. Langston Hughes, *Not Without Laughter* (London: Collier Books, 1969), pp. 292–293.

2. Jones, *Dutchman*, p. 35.

3. Ellison, "Living with Music," p. 189.

4. James Baldwin, "Sonny's Blues," *Going to Meet the Man* (New York: Dell Pub. Co., 1966), pp. 119–122.

5. James Baldwin, *Another Country* (New York: Dell Pub. Co., 1960, 1962), p. 14.

6. Margolies, *op. cit.*, p. 125.

7. James Baldwin, *Blues for Mister Charlie* (New York: Dial Press, 1964), pp. 16–17. All quotations are from this edition.

CHAPTER SIX

The Streetman: The Black Hero as Law Breaker

An altered man
in the sea of a city
in his head he's a dreamer
white women and cars, the rotting artifacts
of lost uncivilizations. His hair is long,
his face round, sometimes soft voice smiles
toward the seat of desire.
> What is the prediction
> of the peoples? What is their pleasure?
> Will they let him live who has sinned
> of his ways? Will they let him breathe
> in the maze he has created, riding
> on his shoulders through the gale
> of his invective. The children
> of his thinking, are stronger
> than he is, will they pity or
> respect, the old old infant.

Amiri Baraka
from "Premises Not Quite Condemned"
Black Magic: Poetry 1961–1967

| I |

The protagonist in *Invisible Man,* who symbolically remains nameless, and Clay, the malleable, who takes his shape and even his coloring from his surroundings until

168

GIVE BIRTH TO BRIGHTNESS

forced to declare himself, are both Black Everymen. Their allegorical dimensions are defined not so much in terms of one clear-cut characteristic, but rather in terms of their use as embodiments of ideas or concepts. One knows them at the end of the book or play more as types than as persons, as ideas rather than individuals. Richard sometimes speaks in the collective voice of Black men, yet his dominant stance, whether singing, shouting, cursing or loving —and he comes across to the audience in all these attitudes—is that of an individual whose life style is refracted through the group experience and in this way becomes universal. Richard learns from the group and becomes stronger even in death because of his reassociation with his people. And it is this circular motion which provides the dominant movement of the play.

By contrast, the movement in *Of Love and Dust* is a straight, forward-rushing motion which moves to a violent, inevitable climax as Marcus, the hero, asserts his independence from those group traditions which limit the ways in which he can define his reality and himself. This kind of assertion is necessary because some of the traditions and customs which have helped Black people survive were forced upon them by a hostile white society, with the view of strangling any impulses toward broader definitions of humanity or manhood. It is a paradox, for the very conventions and laws which were created to stifle, become, when adhered to, a means of survival. The fact that the attempts to debase and degrade Black people have been largely unsuccessful is due to the collective strength of Blacks and also to the fact that individual Blacks have hammered at the rules and conventions which have sought to circumscribe their lives. They have defined themselves in opposition to that group tradition which has sought to overcome white society with "yeses, undermine 'em with grins, agree 'em to death and destruction." This is an alternate mode of expression, a variation on the group/individual pattern, which insures that the traditions which have helped the group survive will not become the cords which also strangle it. The group/individual pattern is not a static one in which the group continually gives strength to its individual members. If the group tradition is to remain viable, if its experience is to be kept alive, the group must also learn and derive strength from its individual members. This is a part of the functions of those rebels and streetmen who throw themselves against the boundaries which whites have attempted to set as the outward limits of Black experience.

In the works of Ernest Gaines, the efforts of the individual to broaden or break out of narrow traditional ways are couched in terms of the conflict between the old and the new. Even though his themes are, in some measure, those which have concerned many Black writers (masculinity, dignity and the effort to align one's personal concept of self with the dominant society's view of one's group identity and experience), his deepest concern is centered on this clash between youth and age, between those who adhere to the patterns which have made it possible for Black people to survive in the past and the young people who are disenchanted with these values. The subsequent attempts of these younger people to erect new values and find new ways of making it through the world provide the framework for many of his stories.

Gaines uses the rural Louisiana countryside as the setting for most of his stories. The countryside and most particularly, the quarters, those ancient structures which have served as homes for generations of Black people back to the times of slavery, are captured in a purposely ill-defined time between the Second World War and the present, a time not quite yesterday, not quite today. The struggle for ascendency in the small Southern backwater Gaines has created is not between white and Black. The racial order, with the Blacks who are on the bottom, rich white people who are on the top and the Cajuns (the descendents of the white Arcadians who were resettled in Louisiana by the British after the close of the French and Indian Wars in the late eighteenth century), who, no matter how high their income, are not quite as good, at least in the eyes of Blacks, as the Anglican whites, but no matter how poor, are at least one step above the Blacks, is slowly changing. But change, in an overtly racial manner, seldom moves beyond the periphery of Gaines's attention. His concern is for the ways in which people attempt to hold on to or break from the past, adjust to the present or influence the future. Thus, his major theme, in its broadest sense, is the clash between the old and the new, the past and the future. The old is violated by the new, not out of wanton destruction; rather it is attacked in an attempt to wrench new definitions, new images of manhood and dignity, new realities out of the old. This is the struggle which comprises the title story from Gaines's volume of short stories, *Bloodline*, for Cooper Laurent, the hero, is determined to claim his birthright from the tradition which has denied him one.

Gaines's older characters seem, at first glance, Faulknerian caricatures who, like the Black servant, Dilsy, in *The Sound and The Fury*, "attempt to hold the white family together . . . [who are] the foundations of a dying institution."[1] Some of the characters are set very firmly in this image but it is a mistake to dismiss any of them as mere stereotypes. There are variations and gradations in Gaines's characterizations. Bishop, in *Of Love and Dust*, for example, blames the troubles of his master, Marshall Hebert, on the convict Marcus. Marcus, literally and figuratively, sticks his foot in the door of the Big House that slavery built, and in Bishop's opinion, a Black person who has the nerve to do that "would do almost anything." Hebert, whom he has served as faithfully as he served the father before him, can do no wrong; he will always be the master to Bishop.

Aunt Margaret, in the same novel, has been nurtured in the same tradition. She acknowledges the guilt of the white overseer, Bonbon, in Marcus' death, but by a willful effort, she refuses to know that Hebert is also implicated in Marcus' death. It is as though this final piece of knowledge must be kept out of her consciousness or she and the racial hierarchy around which she has ordered her life will be swept away in a wind of hurricane force. Or, again, there is old Aunt Fe in "Just Like a Tree" who, on the one hand, accepts, even enjoys, her role of devoted family servant to Anne-Marie Duvall, and on the other, inspires and encourages Emmanuel, the young civil rights worker whose efforts are beginning to stir the quiet backwater of the countryside. Gaines depicts the complexities of the human heart which lie beneath the tragicomic masks his characters often wear.

Gaines's greatest strength as a writer lies in his ability to render, in a believable manner, Black people who are dignified and humane, who find ways of expressing the love and the often fierce tenderness they feel for each other, even though the struggle just to survive demands most of their energies. This is the theme of "The Sky Is Grey." "A Long Day in November" is a joyful noise; the somber, heavy themes of masculine pride and manhood, viewed now from the perspective of a six-year-old boy, are refracted through the tender, lyrically humorous descriptions of the boy's father as the father struggles to keep both pride and family intact.

Of Love and Dust, the chronicle of Marcus Payne, is a community epic. The community is the Marshall Hebert plantation; its heart is the quarters; its nerve center the

Big House. The epic is told through the central voice of
Jim Kelly, a tractor driver on the plantation, who shares
a house with Marcus and, after several false starts, becomes the only friend whom Marcus recognizes. Many
of the events in the story which Jim recounts come to him
in the form of confidences from the other workers on the
plantation who have seen them happen. Jim heads the
chorus of workers whose voices are a counterpoint to
Marcus' actions. These voices emphasize the themes of
identity, masculinity, dignity and the conflict between the
old and the new which are embodied in the actions of the
characters Gaines depicts.

| II |

The hard man-gorilla type of street figure is the model
for the character of Marcus. Like Stagger Lee and John
Henry of folklore and song fame, Marcus does not seek
trouble but he knows how to greet trouble when it comes.
He is a lover who can pull—attract—a woman by merely
looking at her. This kind of pulling power is provocative
and when Marcus attempts to pull the woman of a would-
be hard man, Hotwater, the two men fight. Hotwater draws
a knife and Marcus is forced to kill him in order to save
himself. Instead of going to prison for the killing, Marcus
is bonded out of jail by Marshall Hebert. Hebert has
been persuaded to intervene between Marcus and the law
by Marcus' grandmother. The grandmother, Miss Julie

Rand, had been the Hebert family cook for years. Even though she has been gone from the plantation for a number of years, she still remembers Hebert's complicity in a long-ago murder. She uses this knowledge to get Hebert to bond Marcus out of jail, so that instead of spending five years in the prison at Angola, Marcus is set to spend five years doing manual labor on the Hebert Plantation.

Marcus is a "bad nigger" and his spirit must be broken in order to prove that bad niggers must bow before the will of the white man. It is the task of the Cajun overseer, Sidney Bonbon, to show Marcus that bad niggers are just like other niggers, perhaps a little harder to convince, but convincible, nonetheless. For Bonbon, there is nothing personal in the conflict with Marcus. It is the same conflict he has had with other Black convicts over the years. He has always won because it is part of his job to win. As he tells Jim Kelly, the narrator, near the end of the story:

Me and you—what we is? We little people, Geam [James]. They make us do what they want us to do, and they don't tell us nothing. We don't have nothing to say 'bout it, do we, Geam?[2]

And, because he feels he has nothing to say about it, he becomes the visible instrument of the attempt to dehumanize Marcus.

Bonbon rides a big black stallion each afternoon over to the field where Marcus, along with two other men, is pulling corn. Jim Kelly drives the tractor which pulls the trailer into which the men toss the corn as they pick it.

THE BLACK HERO AS LAW BREAKER

Bonbon rides behind Marcus as Marcus picks and when he falls behind the other men, Bonbon gives him a burlap sack to hang by a rope from his shoulder. Marcus' muscles are already sore from picking and pitching corn; the sack is an added misery for the rope rubs his shoulder raw. Marcus takes this punishment in silence, refusing to ask for mercy or respite. It is not the hard work which infuriates Marcus so much as the fact that Bonbon does not even acknowledge his humanity. He can, as Kelly notes, give Marcus an order and forget about it, secure as he is in the knowledge that Marcus will not talk back, much less strike back.

Marcus has been planning ever since he got to the plantation to run away as soon as his trial—with its prearranged verdict—is over. But as Bonbon continues to drive him, running away is no longer enough for Marcus. He wants some way to strike back at Bonbon, to prove that he is more of a man than the Cajun overseer. He goes after Bonbon's Black concubine, Pauline, but Pauline repulses him. Marcus then turns his eyes toward more dangerous quarry, Bonbon's wife, Louise. The affair between Marcus and Louise begins violently, for each is merely using the other to strike back at Bonbon who has all but abandoned one and continues to torment the other. But these two who had planned only to use each other find that they have come to love one another. Louise needs Marcus' strength and he needs her gentleness. They decide to run away together.

The long-ago crime which Miss Julie used to help Marcus was committed by Bonbon, but instigated by Hebert for the latter's gain. Bonbon has also been using Hebert's complicity in that crime. He steals from Hebert, corn, cotton, cattle, any of the farm produce which he can sell at a profit. By the time the story opens, Bonbon has been taking things from Hebert so long that he no longer feels that he is stealing; he is merely taking what he has a right to. But Hebert is tired of being blackmailed by Bonbon and he wants to get rid of him. Unaware of the affair between Marcus and Bonbon's wife, he offers Marcus his freedom if he will kill Bonbon. Marcus counters with the startling proposal that Hebert help him and Louise to run away. Marcus knows that the taboo against sexual intercourse between a white woman and a Black man is so strong that Bonbon's own family will turn against him and hunt him down if he fails to follow the runaway couple. Marcus is confident that Bonbon will not catch them and the overseer will therefore be unable to return to the plantation. Hebert's purpose can thus be served without bloodshed. This last is important to Marcus for he will kill to defend himself but he is "no hunting dog to go round killing people for nobody else."

Hebert's sense of race wars with his sense of money. Money wins and he says yes to Marcus' plan and further agrees to provide Marcus with a car and a hundred dollars to help the escape. On the night Marcus and Louise plan to run away, Hebert, who is supposed to keep Bonbon occupied, brings him back to the plantation. Bonbon reaches his home just as the pair are descending the steps of the house. In the fight which follows, Bonbon kills Marcus with a scythe and Louise, unable to cope with this new reality, retreats into insanity. There is an inquest, of course, and Bonbon is acquitted and no mention is made of the part Hebert has played.

Bonbon, realizing that he has again been Hebert's murderous instrument, takes Pauline, his Black concubine, their half-breed children and his own child by Louise and leaves the plantation. Hebert is the only winner, for even though most of the Black people on the plantation know that he is responsible for Marcus' death, they are his people. If they speak of his guilt at all, it will only be among themselves.

The bare outline of the plot gives little feeling for the delicately textured fabric which Gaines has woven on this framework. There is force and a driving momentum to the events whose outcome the workers on the Hebert Plantation know is inevitable. But a few, Jim, the narrator, and one or two others, gradually come to hope that Marcus will somehow manage to keep on getting up, that his actions will not produce the inevitable reaction. These perceptive few come to see Marcus as a hero; in him they see an image of what they might have been had they not given in to the rule of the Big House so soon.

Marcus is a product of Baton Rouge's ghetto, and like that of most Black ghettos, its street life is a harsh, often cruel demi-world in which the strongest or the slickest prey upon the weaker, less agile Black people in lieu of preying upon the white man. The situation is compounded by Southern mores which throw the cloak of the white man's protection around a few Blacks, thus giving these few a greater coercive power over their fellows. Marcus was protected from this world until the death of his mother. Then, his father left him with his grandmother and "took off someplace." Marcus, at fifteen, went to work in order to help support himself. On his job at a parking lot, he was victimized by Big Red, who forced Marcus to pay a dollar a day for being "taught the ropes." Marcus, naïvely, complained to the white boss, but "Big Red was his number one nigger and he didn't care what Big Red did." Red charges Marcus an extra dollar a day for having gone to the white man. Then:

I wanted to quit the job, but my nan-nan told me not to. She said the white man would put a bad mark behind my name and it would be hard for me to get another job anywhere else in Baton Rouge. So I stayed there. I stayed there, and every night I prayed. I prayed so much, I even mentioned Big Red's name in church. But instead of me saying, "Jesus, go with Big Red," I said, "Jesus, please make Big Red stop taking my money." When I said that, the church cracked up. Everybody started laughing. Even the preacher on the pulpit. Everybody laughing and coughing and wiping they eyes. Because you see, Jesus didn't do things like that. Jesus healed the sick and raised the dead, but He didn't stop people from taking your money. That wasn't a miracle—not even a little miracle.

The next day when I went to work, Big Red said, "I hear you

been talking 'bout me to a Jew now. That go'n cost you another dollar."

That night he came to collect his three dollars. I had just bought a big bottle of pop.

"All right, pay off," he said. "Don't try to hold back, I'll just go in your pocket."

I paid him off, all right. I splintered that bottle on his head. But 'fore I could move, the law was there hauling me off to jail.

In jail, he is initiated further into the intricacies of street life. He emerges from this experience, hardened, knowing that he has only himself to depend on.

When they let me out of jail, I promised myself I was go'n look out only for myself; and I wasn't go'n expect no more from life than what I could do for myself. And nobody in this world need to expect no more than from me than that.

Thus, he feels no remorse for having killed Hotwater in a fight over Hotwater's own woman. As he says, a man "ought to don't go round with pretty women if he know he can't fight." Marcus has his own personal code and the fight, at least his part of it, was conducted along those lines:

The people [Kelly tells the reader] had made a big circle round him and Hotwater, and, he said, that big sweaty nigger wanted just one thing—his ass. He kept backing away, backing away, and that big nigger kept coming on him. Every time the nigger hit him he went down. After a while he got tired falling and he stood up and started hitting back. He said the nigger was strong and could hit like a mule, but he didn't know anything about covering up. The nigger kept his face unguarded, and he kept his fist in the nigger's face like you keep your fist on one of those little punching bags. . . . So when the nigger saw he couldn't get his face from off his fist, the nigger wanted to change tactics, Marcus said. Now he wanted his knife. But by the time the nigger got out his knife, he had got out his own, too. He said he let the nigger get two good whacks at him (he always believed in playing fair himself); then he threw that knife into the nigger's belly far as he could.

Marcus must, by the very nature of his experience and the codes he has had to internalize as part of surviving in the city, disrupt the visibly structured, backwater world of the Hebert Plantation. The plantation, while akin to the city in its hierarchy—white on the top, Cajun in the middle and Black on the bottom—is a smaller, more closely knit world. The line between basic survival and going under is thin. Even the white man's favor, as in the case of Bonbon and Pauline, can only move one from field to kitchen. One must therefore survive as best one can, with as little harm to others as possible. As James Kelly says of Pauline:

When she first started working in the big house a lot of people in the quarter felt the same way she did: they knew that long as she lived on the plantation she would have to lay with Bonbon if he wanted her to. So why not make the most of it? Why not get out of the hot sun? Why not wear better clothes, why not eat better food? Then there were the other people in the quarter who pretended she was sinning more than any of them had ever done. They did all they could to hurt her, but she took all their insults with a little smile that said, "If he had chose you, where would you be right now?"

Or again, there is Tick-tock, "a single gal in the quarter
. . . she would give you piece if you treated her right. I
[Kelly] had gotten a couple of pieces from her myself.
But we didn't have anything going for us; it was just
friendly. I needed a piece at the time and I asked her for
it and she said yes. I didn't give her any money because
she didn't want any money. But any time I caught her out
somewhere I would buy her a drink . . ." This, too, is
survival; one does the best one can.

The Blacks are prevented from preying too harshly
upon one another by the smallness of their world. If one
gets too far out of line, he is ostracized and the smallness
of the plantation world makes this a serious consideration.
The group tries to ostracize Marcus in order to make him
conform. He does not, however, consider himself a part
of the group, and does not respond to their strictures.
Marcus is only one generation removed from the world
of the Hebert Plantation, but he is still repelled by the
idea of sweating and working in the fields for someone
else's profit. The dirt and sweat tarnish his city image.
The lives of the people in the quarters seem to him to be
bound by the back-breaking labor of the field on one side
and by the white rule of the Big House on the other. Their
existence is too closely akin to that of slaves and his own
urbanity is still new enough that he feels the need of
distinguishing himself from what he feels is the countri-
fied, old-fashioned way of life on the plantation. Marcus'
insistence on wearing his flashy clothes, his refusal to

knuckle under to Bonbon or listen to the staid counsel of Kelly, are as necessary to his image of himself as his black curly hair and his smooth brown skin. If he submits, as do the others in the quarters, to the rule of the Big House, he becomes, in his own mind, little better than a slave.

It is doubly important that Marcus continue to wear his flashy clothes and plan his escape for he has placed himself in another kind of slavery by allowing himself to be bonded out of prison in the first place. The penalty for one Black man killing another in Louisiana in the forties was five years in Angola—a penalty which could be upped at the convenience of any rich and powerful white man, as Hebert reminds Marcus when Marcus refuses to kill Bonbon. Five years as a bond convict on a plantation can be stretched to seven or more years by the time the sentence has been lengthened to make up for runaway attempts and charges at the plantation store. There is also the burden which Gaines describes in his short story, "Three Men," the story of an old man, a young man and a male homosexual in jail. The old man, Munford, tries to get the younger man, Proctor, to refuse to be bonded out by his plantation boss. Munford has been in the same situation and he knows what it has cost him:

"Been going in and out of these jails here, I don't know how long," Munford said. "Forty, fifty years. Started out just like you—kilt a boy just like you did last night. Kilt him and got off—got off scot-free. My pappy worked for a white man who got me off. At first I didn't know why he had done it—I didn't think; all I knowed was I was free, and free is how I wanted to be. Then I got

in trouble again, and again they got me off. I kept on getting in
trouble, and they kept on getting me off. Didn't wake up till I
got to be nearly old as I'm is now. Then I realized they kept
getting me off because they needed a Munford Bazille. They need
me to prove they human—just like they need that thing over
there. [Hattie Brown, the homosexual.] They need us. Because
without us, they don't know what they is—they don't know what
they is out there. With us around, they can see us and they know
what they ain't. They ain't us. Do you see? Do you see how they
think?"

. . . .

"But I got news for them. They us. I never tell them that, but
inside I know it. They us, just like we is ourselves. Cut any of
them open and you see if you don't find Munford Bazille or Hattie Brown there. You know what I mean?"

. . . .

. . . "What I mean is not one of them out there is a man. Not
one. They think they men. They think they men 'cause they got
me and him in here who ain't men. But I got news for them—cut
them open; go 'head and cut one open—you see if you don't find
Munford Bazille or Hattie Brown. Not a man one of them. 'Cause
face don't make a man—black or white. Face don't make him and
fucking don't make him and fighting don't make him—neither
killing. None of this prove you a man. 'Cause animals can fuck,
can kill, can fight—you know that?"

. . . .

". . .It start in the cradle when they send that preacher there to
christen you. At the same time he's doing that mumbo-jumbo
stuff, he's low'ing his mouth to your little nipper to suck out your
manhood. . . .

. . . .

". . . But they don't stop there, they stay after you. If they miss
you in the cradle, they catch you some other time. And when they

catch you, they draw it out of you or they make you a beast—
make you use it in a brutish way. You use it on a woman without
caring for her, you use it on children, you use it on other men,
you use it on yourself. Then when you get so disgusted with
everything round you, you kill. And if your back is strong, like
your back is strong, they get you out so you can kill again." He
stopped and looked at me and nodded his head. "Yeah, that's
what they do with you—exactly. . . . But not everybody end up
like that. Some of them make it. Not many—but some of them
do make it."

. . . .

"Yeah—the pen is one way," he said. "But you don't go to the
pen for the nigger you killed. Not for him—he ain't worth it. . . .
So you don't go to the pen for killing the nigger, you go for yourself. You go to sweat out all the crud you got in your system. You
go, saying. 'Go fuck yourself, Roger Medlow, I want to be a man,
and by God I will be a man. For once in my life I will be a man.' "

"And a month after you been in the pen, Medlow tell them to
kill you for being a smart aleck. How much of a man you is
then?"

"At least you been a man a month—where if you let him get
you out you won't be a man a second. He won't 'low it."[3]

The white man, not knowing who he is, must define
himself against what he isn't and the bad nigger and the
Black homosexual are necessary adjuncts to his negative
definitions. Thus, the Black man who allows himself to
be bonded out of jail by a white boss, willingly, without
understanding the implications of his act, negates his own
humanity. He is no longer his own man and though he
may still play the part of the bad nigger (Munford, even

at his age, will "hit a nigger in the head as quick as I'll look at one"), he has actually surrendered that title, exchanged it for that of "number one nigger." Marcus recognizes this danger. In one of his first exchanges with Kelly, he declares, "They don't nut this kid like they done nut all the rest of y'all round here," and he continually reiterates that he is not "cut out for this." The "this" is not only the hard work but the tightly regimented society in which one's life is bound not only vertically by his color, but horizontally: One can never rise above being Black and all which that implies in the South, and even relationships with other Black people must be predicated upon the wishes of white people.

Marcus is forcibly reminded of the pervasive influence of the white man on the lives of Black people when he tries to talk to Pauline, Bonbon's Black woman. He is first attracted to Pauline because of her beauty and when he learns that she belongs to Bonbon, he is more than ever determined to make her his own. Jim describes the combined effect of Pauline's beauty and her connection with Bonbon on Marcus:

That evening [after first seeing Pauline] he . . . had to drag that sack on his shoulder again, and that black stallion was only about six inches behind him. But he didn't mind at all. He was thinking about Pauline. He was thinking about the sweet words he was going to whisper in her ear. . . . He was going to tell her things Bonbon had never thought about. How could a white man —no, not even a solid white man, but a bayou, catfish-eating Cajun—compete with him when it came to loving.

Marcus knows that he is attractive and he considers himself a great lover. When he calls on Pauline that evening, she is sitting on the gallery with another woman; on the other side of the gallery, separated from them by a wire fence, sit her next door neighbors, Aunt Ca'line and Pa Bully.

"Say what's on your mind, Marcus." [Pauline asks him.]
"I want us to speak by usself," he said.
"Then you better leave," she said.
"You ain't even heard what I had to say."
"If you can't say it in front of Aunt Ca'line and Pa Bully, I don't need to hear it," she said.
"I just want come and see you sometime," he said.
"I didn't hear that," she said. "You can leave."
But he didn't move. He stood there looking at her like he wanted to come closer and touch her. Pauline wore a light green dress that had dark green leaves and red flowers. She looked fresh and pretty sitting there.
"And don't come back, please," she said, "I don't want no trouble."
"They don't have to be no trouble," Marcus said.
"No, they won't be any," she said, getting up. "Good night."

The manner in which Pauline repulses him is galling to his male ego and to his Blackness, for the trouble she speaks of is, of course, with Bonbon. She implies that Marcus is not man enough to handle either Bonbon or the trouble. Marcus tries again the next night and the only words Pauline has for him are "You stay 'way from my house." The next day, Saturday, Bonbon sets Marcus to unloading the corn he has spent all morning pitching and picking. It seems to Marcus that Bonbon is rubbing salt in an open wound, pushing him past the point of endurance, and his rage and resentment mount. The task takes until ten o'clock that night; after cleaning up he goes down to the quarters to the weekly fish-fry. He mets Pauline on the way and as Pa Bully later tells Jim, Marcus refuses to let Pauline pass, even though she asks him to.

"What he got on you?" Marcus said. "What's the matter with you, woman?"

"I'm telling you, let me pass," Pauline said.

"What's the matter with you?" he said. "I been working up there all night like a slave, like a dog—and all on 'count of him. What's the matter with you?"

"I'm telling you," she said. "Let me pass."

He moved closer.

"Don't you put your hands on me," she said. "I mean it, don't you put your hands on me, you killer."

He hit her and knocked her down. She got up.

"If I tell him, he'll kill you for this. He'll kill you."

"You white man bitch," he said. He hit her again. She fell again.

. . . .

Pauline was up again.

"You bitch," Marcus said to her. "You bloody whore."

She was running toward the gate now.

"You whore," he called to her.

Marcus is not just a rejected suitor; he is a Black man who has been rejected by a Black woman in favor of a white man.

Jim tells the reader and her actions later in the novel

indicate that Pauline loves Bonbon or at least cares deeply for him. Yet, her rejection of Marcus is always stated in terms of staying out of trouble. One feels that had she told Marcus that she remained faithful to Bonbon because she loved him, and not because she was afraid of him or afraid of what he might do if she took another lover, her rejection of Marcus, while still painful, would at least have given some recognition to his masculinity. As it is, he feels that Pauline has failed to pay even the barest recognition to his masculinity and his rage at her increases his hatred of Bonbon.

All of this becomes a part of Marcus' rebellion. In this context, the white woman, Louise, is at once central and peripheral. She is central because historically and traditionally one of the most dangerous and therefore one of the most courageous ways in which a Black man could prove his masculinity was through the sexual conquest of a white woman. Certainly, it is a telling blow against the Southern caste system. Marcus, assaulted on one side by Bonbon who would reduce him to the status of a chattel slave or number one nigger, and by Pauline who cannot even see these possibilities in him, and on the other by Jim who wants him to realize and accept the consequences of his actions, accept the responsibilities of his own humanity and masculinity, must make a definitive move which tells the world—and himself—just who he really is.

He is fighting Bonbon for his life but because of his

friendship with Jim, he must prove that he is a man and human. It is precisely because he feels that Pauline has not treated him as a man that he is driven into Louise's arms. After Pauline's second rejection of him:

He thought how he would be a completely different person with [Pauline's] lovely body . . . to come home to. Then he realized that that body was for a white man, and he got mad again. He wanted to hurt her. He wanted to really hurt her. But how? Beat her up? Kill one of her children? Yes, yes, that would hurt her. But what would that do to Bonbon? Probably nothing. What did Bonbon care about two little mulatto children? . . .

How could he hurt Bonbon? How? How? Wait; wait. Yes— sure. Bonbon had a wife too, remember. Yes, that's right, he had a wife. And some kind of way he would get to his wife. So let them lynch him—let them. What did he care.

And Jim retells the meeting with Pauline, this time from Marcus' point of view:

. . . after taking a bath and coming outside, who should he see in the road but Pauline, walking by herself. He said if she had acted toward him the way a woman ought to act toward a man, everything about Bonbon's wife would have been forgotten. But, no, when she saw him she acted like she had seen the devil himself. He said that's why he hit her. He wanted to show her he was a man, not dirt. He said he was so mad with her he wanted to kill her, and yet, at the same time, if she had given him a little smile, he would have been ready to kill Bonbon for her.

Louise is peripheral because Marcus has been placed in a situation which will make him or break him and the instrument of his making is almost incidental. Pauline could just as easily have taken Louise's place in Marcus' life, just as she had already taken Louise's place in Bonbon's life.

Where Marcus sees the woman in Pauline first and only later considers her possibilities as an instrument of revenge, Louise enters his life as nothing more than a tool.

> . . . he wanted her only for revenge. He wanted to get to her, not her getting to him. He wanted to clown for her, he probably would have stood on his head for her, probably would have walked on his hands for her- until he got into those drawers. Then that would have been the end. If they lynched him after, it wouldn't have meant a thing. Because, you see, they couldn't take away what he had got. No. he probably would have laughed at his lynchers.

Louise is a strange, childlike creature. Forced into a marriage at fifteen, she has grown to hate her brutish husband and wants only to leave him. During the early years of her marriage, she ran away several times and each time her father and brothers, cruder, more brutish versions of her husband, brought her back. She does not hate Pauline for being her husband's mistress, for receiving the love which legally should have been hers. She does hate the fact that Pauline is Black and therefore cannot marry Bonbon. Their marriage would free her and that is what she wants: freedom and revenge.

> Bonbon would have to pay. Pay for the suffering she had gone through while he slept in Pauline's bed; pay for the suffering she had gone through on that bayou with her brothers and papa.

But Louise didn't know how to get revenge. She didn't have any idea what she was going to do, Aunt Margaret said. She was twenty-two now, had given birth to a child, but she was still a child herself. She hadn't learned anything about being a woman from her papa and brothers . . . and Bonbon hadn't taught her anything, either. So she didn't know how a woman got revenge. . . .

. . . by watching Pauline, Louise knew how she would get her revenge. Only she didn't know if she could go through with it. She would have to practice awhile, she would have to build up her courage. . . . what she needed courage for was to put herself in a man's way to make him look at her. Because, Aunt Margaret said, she didn't know if she had anything worth looking at. Since Bonbon never looked at her, she wasn't too sure anybody else would look at her, either. . . .

Then she put it to the test. She started sitting on the gallery watching. If she got the right look she was going to make her move. She didn't care if he could or he couldn't, she just wanted him to touch her. She wanted a mark on her flesh. She had to have proof, she had to have a mark. You had white women who had just said it and had had a nigger lynched; you had some who had dreamed it and had had a nigger lynched; others had done it themselves and had had a nigger lynched; but Louise needed the mark. Because she wasn't sure she had anything worthwhile, and she was afraid if she hollered rape everybody might laugh at her. But with a mark, Bonbon would definitely have to kill the nigger. Marshall Hebert would definitely get rid of Bonbon for the stealing that he had been doing—and she would be free to leave.

By the time Marcus comes along, she has been sitting on the gallery three years, trying to entice, with her eyes, any of the men on the plantation. None of the men have been willing to risk death in order to sleep in her bed. After his rejection by Pauline, Marcus finally notices Louise and sees the invitation—and the challenge—in her eyes. For three nights he stands outside the fence surrounding Bonbon's house and attempts to talk with Louise. Her only response is a dreamy look. But the next Saturday, Marcus is set, at Louise's request, to raking the leaves in her yard. By this time, Jim, who has, in spite of himself, become Marcus' friend and counselor, knows what Marcus has in mind. He warns Aunt Margaret, the housekeeper/cook in the Bonbon household, not to leave Louise and Marcus alone together.

But neither Bonbon's faithful dog or the watchful eye of Aunt Margaret is enough to stop Marcus:

She hadn't been ironing a minute [Aunt Margaret told Kelly] when she heard a loud, booming noise in Louise's bedroom. She jumped around and faced the door, then she went to the door and asked Louise what was the matter. Louise didn't answer. Aunt Margaret heard another noise: it sounded like two people moving fast and trying to be quiet at the same time.

"Wait," Aunt Margaret said. "I know this ain't what I think it is."

Marcus has climbed through Louise's bedroom window and the two are joined in a noisy chase which ends in Louise's capture on the bed:

She heard something slam against the wall—it sounded like a piece of furniture.

"What was that?" she called. "What hit there?"

Nobody answered. Then she heard the same noise again. It might have been a chair one of them was throwing against the wall.

Aunt Margaret moved back to hit the door with her shoulders. She said she knew that the little frail latch would fly off even if Tite [Louise's child] had hit that door hard enough. She hit it.

But like she had hit one of those oak trees out in the yard, she went falling back on the floor. . . .

"So that's it, that's what she was doing," Aunt Margaret said. "Propping things back there."

"Come out of there, boy," Aunt Margaret hollered through the door. "You hear me?"

She said one of them slammed that chair against the wall again. She said she tried to vision what chair it was, but she didn't have time for visioning. . . . Just about then that chair or something else heavy slammed against the wall. Then it got quiet—too quiet.

"What y'all doing?" Aunt Margaret said softly, holding her ear against the door. "Miss Louise, what y'all doing in there?"

Then she heard another loud, booming noise, like somebody had jumped from one end of the room to the other. Marcus said:

"I got you now, I got you now, you pretty little hot pretty thing. I got you now, hanh? Hanh? Give me my two little pears here. Give 'em here. Give me my two little sweet pears."

. . . .

She heard a slap.

"What was that?" she called, and listened. "What was that? You slapped that white woman, boy?"

She said she heard "Why you pretty little hot—you taking it off or I'm go'n tear it off?"

"She ain't go'n do nothing and you neither," Aunt Margaret said through the door. "Not long as I can draw breath."

. . . .

Marcus was saying, "Lord, look how pretty you is. Lord, I didn't know you was this pretty. How can a man leave all this pretty goodness and go—Oh, Lord, look at all this. And look at my two little pears hanging there, just look at 'em."

Aunt Margaret hit the door and hit it again.

She heard Marcus saying, "Now see me, see how pretty I'm is. See that? See?"

"Boy, you naked in there?" Aunt Margaret called through the door. "You naked in there, boy?"

"Let me kiss you," he said. "Oooooo, you sweet. Good Lord— Lord have mercy. He know you this sweet? Let me kiss this little pear here . . . now this one. Two of the sweetest little pears I ever tasted. 'Specially this one here . . . Go on touch it. That's right, touch it. Won't hurt you. See? See?"

Aunt Margaret hit the door again. She hit it again, again, again. Then she heard him laughing. She figured he was carrying Louise to the bed, because the next sound she heard was the spring when they lay down. She pushed against the door again— not with her shoulder—with both hands. But she knew it was no use. And even if she had got into the room, it would have been too late now. She could tell by the deep moan that Louise made.

There is a certain naïveté and innocence about Marcus' obvious satisfaction in his own sexuality and sensuousness, in his invitation to Louise to delight in him as he does in her. Marcus awakens and challenges Louise's feminine sexuality and her response to him makes her a woman, gives birth to a womanliness which neither marriage nor motherhood has engendered. They move from this first sexual encounter which is almost a fight—but not a rape—to a deadly serious hide-'n-seek-like game played under the trees:

The window was opened so Aunt Margaret could still see Marcus and Louise in the yard. . . . They played out there like two children who didn't have a thing in the world to hide. Aunt Margaret said Marcus ran around the oak tree, and Louise broke for the pecan tree a few feet away. Marcus ran there, and Louise ran to the oak tree again. Marcus ran there, and Louise broke across the yard. Marcus caught up with her and tripped her down, but she kicked and wiggled until she was free and running again. He jumped up, caught up with her, and tripped her again. She kicked herself free. All this time the dog was barking   running from one end of the small yard to the other end, barking. Marcus jumped up and caught up with Louise and tripped her down again. This time he kept her there. Aunt Margaret watched them tussling and rolling over and over. Then they stopped. They lay quietly, side by side, holding each other, kissing each other.

They invite discovery, almost ask that someone betray them. Again Louise is the chased, Marcus the chaser, but now the challenge is to Marcus' masculinity. Louise seems to imply by her light-hearted romp from tree to tree that Marcus must do twice as much as a white man in order to be good enough for her. Marcus rises to the challenge and puts all thought of personal danger out of his mind and concentrates on her, on winning and loving the prize of her body. The capture at the end of the chase is two-fold. Marcus captures Louise's body—a foregone conclusion, really—but he also captures her deepest emotions. After this game under the trees, Louise asks Aunt Margaret if "a white girl can love a nigger. . . . I mean a nig-gro." But the quietness, the unhurried tenderness with which Marcus makes love to Louise in this exposed and dangerous spot is also indicative of Marcus' own entrapment; she takes his body into hers and she takes his heart.

The nude chase is folly on Marcus' part. Yet even in participating in so foolish an action, he proves conclusively that he is more than equal to any challenge which the white woman can issue. In this, he seems larger than life and his fall, his death, at the end of the novel is earth-shattering.

Marcus falls from the only promontory which a street-man considers worthy of climbing, that of controlling any game which he tries to run on others. In loving Louise, he loses sight of his reasons for having her. Pauline and Bonbon are forgotten in his realization that he has a heart which can love. He shows Louise just how nice a man can be. In doing so, he loses control of his game, but control is traded for proof that he is both a man and human. His deceptively cool front gives way before the power of his love for Louise, as well as his love, and most importantly, his respect for James Kelly. These two forces are central to the growth which Marcus experiences during the course of the novel.

⎱ III ⎰

Miss Julie Rand has laid the charge of looking after her grandson on Jim. Jim accepts because he, as Marcus says, cares for everybody. The friendship between the two men starts out on rocky ground. Marcus thinks that Jim is a whitemouth, an Uncle Tom without "nuts." Jim knows that Marcus is a hard-headed hard man, a playboy who, despite his insistence to the contrary, has a lot to learn in the world. As he says, "I wanted to feel sorry for Marcus, but God knows he didn't help you." Marcus, of course, does not want his pity. The two curse and insult

each other, but they still create a friendship which enriches both. Marcus comes to see Jim as a man who "cares
for everybody" yet has managed to keep more than a little
of his masculinity and self-respect. He will never make
it, in Marcus' terms, never show that wild, irresponsible
daring of which Marcus is capable, yet Marcus comes to
love and rely on Jim for the quiet strength and humanity
which everyone in the quarters, including Bonbon, re-
spects.

The delicate threads of their friendship are almost
broken by Marcus' relationship with Louise. Jim is afraid
for Marcus and the others on the plantation because if
Marcus is caught, he and perhaps half the people on the
plantation will pay in blood for that relationship. When
talking to Marcus brings no results, Jim and the older
people retreat into silence, hoping to bring Marcus to his
senses by this means. The only thing, however, which gives
Marcus pause is Hebert's offer to help him escape, if
Marcus will kill Bonbon. In a deeply moving and poignant
scene, Marcus turns to Jim for the advice he has so often
spurned:

"Speak to you?" Marcus said.
  . . . He sat down at the table. He had been out of the field two
or three hours, but he still hadn't washed his hands or his face.
I could see the dirt on his face and the rings of dirt around his
neck. His pink shirt had brown sweat stains around the armpit
and on the shoulder where he had been dragging the sack.
  Marcus sat at the table fumbling with his cap. This was the first
time we had sat down together in over a week. He didn't know

how to start the conversation. He passed his tongue over his lips and started to say something, then he fumbled with the cap again.

"Can I have a beer—if you got one?" he said.

"I had a couple of bottles in the icebox. I got them out and gave him one. I sat back at the table with the other bottle.

Marcus drank and set the bottle on the table. He was still looking at the bottle instead of me. He started to say something, but he raised the bottle to his mouth again.

"We been talking," he said.

I didn't say anything. He raised his head and looked at me.

"We think we getting to like each other some," he said.

I still didn't say anything to him. Just waiting. Both of us knew he was going to make me mad.

"Maybe a lot," he said.

"I suppose you mean you and Louise, Marcus?"

He nodded. "Yeah."

"Well, what are you telling it to me for?"

"You the only friend I got, Jim."

I shook my head. "I'm not your friend, Marcus. I was stuck with you. That old lady in Baton Rouge stuck you on me. I'm not your friend."

He didn't hear a word I said. Even when I was talking I could see he wasn't listening. He raised the bottle to his mouth and set it back again.

"She want leave from here," he said. "She want me get her 'way from here."

"Then do it," I said. "There's a bus running out there twice a day."

·   ·   ·   ·   ·   ·   ·   ·   ·   ·   ·   ·   ·   ·   ·

He looked at me awhile, then he started wiping the frost of the bottle with the side of his finger.

"We go'n need help," he said.

"Did you ask Bonbon?"

"No, but Marshall say he'll do it."

He had raised his head and he was looking straight at me because he knew how that was going to hit me. . . .

"He asked me when I was go'n run. I told him I wasn't go'n run. He said if I didn't Bonbon was go'n kill me in the field. If I got him first there might be a car and some money waiting."

"You're lying, Marcus."

"Why you think he bond me out? You think he care anything for nan-nan?"

"Yes; because she told me so. She told me that night when I took you to Baton Rouge; she told me the other Sunday when she came here. Yes, I believe that's why he got you out. Yes, Marcus."

"Well, you wrong, and she wrong. He got me out to kill Bonbon. He got something 'gainst Bonbon or Bonbon got something 'gainst him, and he want Bonbon out the way." Marcus stopped and looked at me. His eyes were sad. I didn't know his eyes could get so sad. But I supposed it was like that with anybody who tried to be tough all the time. "I ain't no dog, Jim," he said. "I killed that nigger 'cause that nigger was go'n kill me. But I ain't no hunting dog to go round killing people for nobody else."

. . . .

"Is that what you been thinking about doing, Marcus?"

"I been thinking 'bout plenty things," he said. "I know now I got to get 'way from here and get 'way from here soon."

"Don't try that, Marcus."

"I can't stay here ten years, Jim."

"It's five—that's if you're guilty, Marcus."

"He say I'm already guilty and it's ten. They changed all the rules the day after I killed that nigger."

"He's just pushing you, Marcus. He's doing it to see what you'll do. If you don't bite for this bait, he'll leave you alone and try somebody else."

"It's not just him. I got to get 'way from here for myself. If I don't Jim, I'm go'n get in plenty more trouble. I know that."

"If you try this, Marcus, you'll really get in trouble," I said.

. . . .

"Sooner or later, Jim, I got to try," he said "I got to get 'way from here."

"It won't work, Marcus," I told him again. "You'll need money, you'll need food, you'll need a car. It won't work. You'll just end up in Angola."

"I can't stay here ten years, Jim," he said. He was getting mad now and his voice was getting high. "I can't even stay here ten weeks," he said.

"You can if you make up your mind to do it, Marcus," I said. "If you try, if you try hard. And I'll be around here— I don't know how long—but I'll be here. I'll do all I can to—"

"I can't stay here," he screamed at me now. "Can't you see I can't stay here. Can't you see I ain't like that. Can't you see . . ."

Jim finally does see, but too late to tell Marcus. Bonbon has already killed him with a scythe by the time Jim comes to recognize the significance of Marcus' actions. The realization hits him as he works in the fields on the day of Marcus' planned departure:

I admired Marcus. I admired his great courage. . . . I wanted to tell him how brave I thought he was. He was the bravest man knew, the bravest man I had ever met. Yes, yes, I wanted to tell him that. And I wanted to tell Louise how I admired her bravery. I wanted to tell them that they were starting something—yes, that's what I would tell them; they were starting something that others would hear about, and understand, and would follow.

That "something others would hear about, and understand" is not miscegenation but the crumbling of the Big House and the caste system, that traditional pattern of actions and reactions with which whites have attempted to dehumanize and emasculate Black people.

Kelly comes to symbolize the uneasy ground between past and future. For him, it is always "one day, one day." One day, he will assert himself, assert the strength that has carried him and his people through the years, declare himself in opposition to the rule of the Big House so that no longer will he be reduced to a status only a little removed from that of a tool. As he says of the "nigger room" in the plantation store where Black people must drink their beer if they want to drink it on the premises:

I kept telling myself, "One of these days I'm going to stop this, I'm going to stop this; I'm a man like any other man and one of these days I'm going to stop this." But I never did. Either I was too thirsty to do it, or after I had been working in the field all day I was just too tired and just didn't care.

Unlike Bishop, Hebert's servant, who accepts the Big House's rule out of a profound belief that it is right, Jim does so because he cannot take the chance of discovering that whatever he erects in its place will be little better than what he has helped to destroy. Marcus accuses him, near the end of the story, of being old-fashioned. "Where [he asks] would people be if they didn't take a chance? You know where? Right here. Right here in this quarter the rest of their life." The quarter for Marcus is slavery and he would rather die—and does—before agreeing that this is all he is suited for. Jim is bereft of belief: "I looked at Marcus and I felt empty inside. I felt empty because he could not believe in friendship or God; I felt empty because I doubted if I believed in anything either." He comes to understand that the same fear which keeps the other people of the quarters in their houses on the night that Marcus plans to run away with Louise is the same fear which has also held him. "It was the same fear that made me hate Marcus at first. It was fear for myself and the rest. The fear was still in me, but I didn't blame Marcus any more. Because it wasn't Marcus who was doing it; it was the big people."

Implicit throughout the story is the idea that Jim loves Pauline but, believing that she loves Bonbon, he makes no effort to engage her affections. This may be an excuse for his own lack of initiative; it is more likely that Jim's love for Pauline is selfless enough that he does not wish to cause her trouble—which is perhaps an acknowledgement that, unlike Marcus, he feels incapable of handling that trouble, should it come. He accompanies Pauline and Bonbon into Baton Rouge without complaint, even though he realizes that he is along only to put a respectable front on the lovers' escapade. He finally draws the line at securing a room for Pauline and Bonbon. But his stand is almost too little too late, for his very act of accompanying the two that far has belittled and demeaned his masculinity in his own eyes. And finally, he realizes that he, at thirty-three, is more Past than anything else. "[I looked at Aunt Margaret] 'I'll be like this one day,' I thought. 'But Marcus never would have been like this.'"

IV

Some of the situations in the story, as Hoyt Fuller observes, are classics in Black experience in America.[4] Their constant repetition makes them now seem almost as much stereotype or myth as fact or reality. Gaines has taken these situations and woven them into a cloth which is textured in design, rich in meaning. The white overseer and his Black concubine and the love which makes the white man forget about his wife waiting at home is one such situation. As Jim Kelly tells it:

It had started in the field, where [Bonbon] had all the right to call [Pauline] over into a patch of corn or cotton or cane or the ditch—the one he was closest to—and make her lay down and pull up her dress. Then after he had satisfied his lust, he would get back on the horse like nothing had happened. And she would pull down her dress and go back to the work she was doing before he had called her to him. The other women wouldn't say anything to her, and she wouldn't say anything, either—like nothing in the world had happened.

These first encounters are vulgar and animalistic and if Pauline is not completely degraded by her intercourse with Bonbon, it is because she manages to remain spiritually aloof from the uses to which her body is put. But, as later happens with Marcus and Louise, love enters through the door opened by lust.

. . . something had happened to Bonbon. At first he had laid with all and any of them. When his lust was up he had called the one closest to him. But after being with so many, now he settled for one. . . .

Bonbon was in love with Pauline . . . but it took years for Pauline to fall in love with Bonbon. She didn't want to fall in love with this white man because she knew nothing good could come of it. She knew she would have to be his woman long as she lived on the plantation and long as he wanted her, but she didn't want to hold any feeling for him at all. She wanted it to be "come and go" and nothing else. She figured that after a while it would come to an end, anyhow.

But it didn't come to an end. . . .

After so many years, Pauline did fall in love with Bonbon. She couldn't help but fall in love with him. She knew he loved her more than he did his wife up the quarter or his people who lived on the river.

So now the [corn] shuck mattress [which had been noisy beneath the battle of their lust] was quiet.

But here the situation becomes less classic. By contrasting Bonbon with Marcus and their interrelated love affairs, Gaines points up the weakness of one by emphasizing the strength of the other. The two men are caught up in traditions and codes which seem beyond their control. Bonbon achieves a measure of freedom within the confines of his tradition by cheating Marshall Hebert of whatever he can and obtaining Hebert's acquiescence by threatening to expose his complicity in the old murder. But Bonbon never questions the order of things; it is right that Hebert can require him to kill just as it is right that he drive Marcus until Marcus breaks. Marcus cannot accept a code or tradition which requires that he be no more than a dehumanized part in it, and the minute he steps onto the plantation he comes into conflict with all those who would try to make him play that part.

THE BLACK HERO AS LAW BREAKER

Both men, too, find love outside their proscribed boundaries. Bonbon accepts the fact that marriage between a white man and a Black woman is not looked upon with favor in his world. He attempts to achieve what happiness, what togetherness he can without violating the stricture against interracial marriage. And Pauline accepts the idea that she and Bonbon can never marry just as she has accepted the idea that she had to be Bonbon's woman for as long as he wanted her. Marcus and Louise violate the even stronger sanction against sexual intercourse between a white woman and a Black man, yet neither is willing to allow customs and traditions which are essentially dehumanizing to continue to define their lives in this manner. It is not so much an act of courage for them to meet sexually as it is an act of courage for them to run away together. Bonbon pays an oblique tribute to this courage when he gives Marcus the opportunity to run. Jim relates Bonbon's feelings when he realizes that Marcus and Louise are daring what he could not:

[Bonbon] told me he didn't want to fight Marcus, he was hoping that Marcus would run from him. If Marcus had made any attempt to run, he would have let him go, and there wouldn't have been a thing said about it. But when Marcus didn't run, he had to fight him. Not just fight him, but he had to kill him. If he hadn't killed Marcus, he would have been killed himself. The Cajuns on the river would have done that.

Even recognizing Marcus' attempt to break away from those inhuman traditions based on pride and fear, Bonbon chooses to remain faithful to the code which condemns him to snatching secret moments instead of living an open life with the Black woman he loves.

Marcus never articulates the reason or the significance of his deeds just as he never defines the reason for any of his acts of small rebellion, beyond a "I'm not cut out for this life," or "They don't nut this kid." He simply knows that in order to be a man in his own eyes he must continue to define himself in his own terms, without regard to whether or not his definitions are agreeable with orders from the Big House. Thus, in that brief moment when he has the chance to run away, leaving Louise, he cannot do anything but stay, for otherwise he concurs with, submits to the order which he has been fighting most of his life. He fights Bonbon because of Louise; he dies because of Louise. She is the agent who inspires him to this final declarative act. But n the last fight with Bonbon he fights *for* what he has fought for all along: himself and his life. In choosing to fight Bonbon, he declares that it is not in the power of the white man to give him a way out. He dies for the right to define his own ways out, and in.

It is significant that this struggle takes place on the level of the "little" men. It is presided over, however, by the shadowy figure of the man in the Big House. Hebert seems removed, aloof from the tragedy which has been played out in his backyard. But Marcus has also stuck his foot in the door of that house and Gaines implies that, as a result, this door can never be closed securely again.

The cast of minor characters and their individual responses to the situations Marcus generates partake, in lesser and greater degrees, of the classic. Many of these characters dislike Marcus: Aunt Margaret cannot even bring herself to speak to him. Most of them fear the consequences of his actions: Bishop is appalled that Marcus actually has the nerve to stick his foot in the door which has been closed against him and force his way into the Big House which slavery built. A very few admire him: Charlie Jordan, one of the field hands, sits on his gallery the day Marcus plans to leave, peering at Marcus' house across the way, trying to store up these last glimpses of the man who has become a hero, a source of pride, for him. Most of the plantation people know of Marcus' affair with Louise; all know of his plan to run away with her because he has told them. But no one betrays him, for like him or not, he is their hard man. Having done all they could to dissuade him, they will do nothing further to endanger him.

There are the faithful family servants, both active and retired: Miss Julie Rand, Marcus' grandmother, who uses her knowledge of Hebert's past in order to have her grandson from the prison at Angola; Aunt Margaret, who takes care of Bonbon's little girl but who gives her loyalty to the Hebert family because they have always been the masters her family served; and Bishop, the old servant in the Big House who prays that Marshall Hebert and his house will be protected from Marcus and the future he represents. And there are the field hands, who apparently have become inured to the way things "is," who accept the order which white people have prescribed and do not even, as Marcus comments, "chunk on [their] houses at night."

There is also Jim, the narrator of this tale. He is steadfast and loyal, walking the precarious line between small defeats, small humiliations and even smaller triumphs and declarations. In life, as in the story, he is more observer than participant. Yet his character is the standard by which one measures Marcus and only after one is deep into the story is it apparent that, for all his strength and other admirable traits, Jim is not really a big enough man to measure Marcus by.

The final situation, which combines at once fear and desire, is the Black man who tests or proves his masculinity by flaunting the taboo against a Black man having sexual intercourse with a white woman. The design is old, but Marcus sweeps like a raw abrasive wind through the tapestry Gaines has created, changing—at best—a few lives but sowing seeds which must blossom at a future date and destroy the design which the past has tried so hard to preserve.

Notes: Chapter 6

1. Addison Gayle, Jr., "Cultural Hegemony: The Southern White Writer and American Letters," *Amistad*, I (Feb. 1970), p. 20.

2. Ernest Gaines, *Of Love and Dust* (New York: Bantam Books, 1967), p. 252. All quotations are from this edition.

3. Ernest Gaines, "Three Men," *Bloodline* (New York: Dial Press, 1969), pp. 137–138, 140–141.

4. Hoyt Fuller, "Books Noted," *Negro Digest* (Nov. 1967), pp. 51–52, 85.

Conclusion *A Thematic Study in Neo-Black Literature*

we run the dangercourse
the way of the stocking caps & murray's grease
(if u is modern u used duke greaseless hair pomade)
jo jo was modern /an international nigger
                              born: jan 1, 1863 in new york mississippi
his momma was mo militant than he was /is
jo jo bes no instant negro
his development took all of 106 years
& he was the first to be stamped "made in USA"

.   .   .   .

we *ran* the dangercourse.
now, it's silent walk/a careful eye.
jo jo is there
to his mother he is unknown
(she accepted with a new look: what wd u do if someone
                                        loved u?)
jo jo is back
& he will catch all the new jo jo's as they wander in & out
and with a fan-like whisper say:
                you ain't no
                tourist
                and Harlem ain't for
                sight-seeing, brother.

Don L. Lee
from "We Walk the Way of the New World"
We Walk the Way of the New World

It is, of course, an exaggeration to say that the Black villain in the white community is the hero of the Black community. Rather, it is more accurate to say that a hero in the eyes of Black people is more likely to be a law breaker than a law-maker. Beyond the simple fact that it is only recently that even a small number of Black people have been in a position to affect and effect rules which touch the lives of Blacks, is the deeper, more significant fact that laws have been used more as instruments for the oppression of Black people than as means to serve or protect them. And, where the judicial system has been lax in controlling Blacks, social customs have taken up the slack. Thus, obtaining the dominant society's approval for public or private actions has not been, for Blacks, to obey the laws and be considered a respectable, law-abiding man, but to obey the laws and be praised as a good nigger. It is thus almost axiomatic that good niggers cannot be heroes, for heroes affirm through their actions not only the values of their culture but also their personal worth in their own eyes. The Black man, in being one, must always fail in the other. American history provides glaring instances in which Blacks have sought a white-defined heroism only to find that they have negated their own humanity. The Black betrayers of the revolt plots of Vesey and Prosser are prime examples, for these trusted and confidential servants of slave masters said through their acts of betrayed heroism that it was their place and the place of other Blacks to remain in perpetual servitude to the white man.

The street people, whom whites view as crooks, thugs and cheats, move around and through and against these soul destroying laws and customs and their actions are self-affirming and self-defining feats which other Blacks applaud, admire and imitate. Black people have seen a vision of their own humanity mirrored in these bad men. Even the use of a term like bad men—or any of a number of increasingly vulgar appellations (in the estimation of whites)—to describe an admirable and imitated figure is indicative of the way in which Blacks have had to wrest positive meaning from the Anglo-American lexicon, which provides only the most negative descriptive terms for Black people. For to be a bad man is to be, above all, a man who acts and who deals with the consequences of his actions. The bad man, then, is the hero in the Black communities of the land.

Throughout the course of this work, the term "Black hero" has been used in a limited and specialized sense to symbolize the distinctive fusion of rebellion and group consciousness which characterizes some of the central male figures—the streetmen—in Neo-Black literature. As in much contemporary European and American fiction, the protagonist is in rebellion against society. In Neo-Black fiction, however, society is always the dominant white society which oppresses and suppresses the humanity of Black people and their strivings toward positive self-definitions. The white man as aspiring hero has seldom been required to deny his humanity in order to achieve heroic status. Even in rebellion against his culture, the white man is distinguished from the rebellious Black man by the fact that his status as an outsider hinges upon his personal questioning of or quarrel with the world in which he lives. Were it possible for him to resolve this quarrel in terms which his world would find acceptable, he would be welcomed back into the sheepfold like any other lost lamb. The Black man faces a different situation, for whatever his internal adjustment to the values of the white society, it is impossible for him to adjust the color of his skin, the look of his facial features or the texture of his hair so that they coincide with the physical characteristics which this society values. Black skin, thick lips and noses and kinky hair mark him as a ravening untamed beast, not a domesticated animal. On another level, the situation of the central character in Kafka's *The Trial* is an alarmingly lifelike metaphor. The situation in *Native Son* is fictionalized reality and the hound which pursues and finally captures Bigger Thomas captures thousands of Black men, even now in the last half of the twentieth century, simply because they are Black. Thus, while Clay and Walker may sit beside the white anti-heroes and picaros of Western tradition, they can never be fully at ease in this company; they can never make enough tracks to cover the distance to that side of the fence. Their skin will always betray them.

Estrangement and isolation are the central characteristics of the anti-heroic figures in Western literature and
they stand in marked contrast to what ultimately becomes
an intregal part of the streetman's characterization in Neo-
Black literature: the reintegration of the street hero with
the tradition and culture of Black people on both a meta-
phoric and a concrete level. But even before this reintegration takes place, the alienation of the streetman differs
from that of similar figures in Western culture. While all
these figures are alienated from the dominant society, the
streetman is wedded to the Black subculture in dual relationships. One aspect of the duality lies in the estrangement which Black people feel toward that part of themselves which is bound up in slavery and segregation, in
the seeming docility, punctuated by briefly flaring violence, which has characterized the history of Black people
in America. Degradation of humanity and castration of
masculinity override the deep wellsprings of endurance
and dormant power which the merest survival in the racist
climate of America must also symbolize. And while Black
people do not wish to see themselves in that history, they
must see themselves there, for Black is an unyielding knot
which ties them to the first Africans who stepped off the
ship at Jamestown to become the first Black slaves in the
United States. Thus, the streetman attempts to forge in the
present what he feels has been left unmade in the past: a
powerful heroic image. The streetman is also integrated
into the Black community in an almost parasitic unity,

deriving both his status and often his income from the Black world in which and upon which his feats are performed. Yet the existence of the streetman in Black experience is more than just tolerated. His actions, whether directed against whites or Blacks, are looked upon as community epics in which all can vicariously partake of the thrill of action and achievement. It is this relationship, the interdependency of the one upon the other, which allows for the future redemption, the rechanneling of the driving strength of the streetman into directions which are less self—and community—destroying. The relationship is thus placed upon a mutually constructive plane. The streetman retains his heroic image but he becomes a community resource in much the same way in which the community has been his personal resource. This resolution to isolation and end to estrangement in Neo-Black literature is seldom paralleled in the literature of the picaro or the anti-hero. The only resolution left these Western characters is a personal one which finds no echoing response in their cultures.

The reintegration of the streetman with his origins strips him of that lone-wolf posture with its emphasis on the control and manipulation of others for his own personal gain, and renders him loving and lovable, strengthened and able and willing to share his strength. It is this aspect of reciprocity which conclusively separates the street-wise Black hero from the ranks of anti-heroes or picaros. Indeed, to even try to examine or interpret the streetmen in Neo-Black literature in this light is to obscure the central features of their character. The streetman must be defined in terms of the Black experience and that thematic current in Black literature which sees Black history and Black heritage as a source of regenerative strength rather than an instance of humiliating weakness.

| II |

The white woman is a recurring figure in each of the works under discussion. This is not incidental: to speak about the Black man in literature is almost always to speak about the white woman. As the object of an almost always illicit desire and the butt of ribald, taunting jokes, the white woman is one of the most traditional figures in the culture and history of Black people in America. The relationship between this woman and the Black heroes takes on an almost ritualistic quality, for the literary portrayal seems almost always designed to evoke visions of power and masculinity. One says 'this woman' for in Black literature she is always the same, a symbol devoid of human warmth or feeling, sometimes, as in *Of Love and Dust*, almost devoid of sense, until the deep warmth and earthiness that is Black touches and awakens her. Most often she is so sterile or calculating that even contact with Black reality cannot reclaim her. She recoils in fear with cries of rape— for warmth will rape, will pillage the cold of its power —as does Jo Britten. Or, she becomes a Lula who attacks and destroys the presence which might have given her light. Whatever guise she takes, the white woman almost always represents a challenge, a gauntlet flung in the face of the Black man's masculinity. To refuse the challenge is to admit that one is somehow lacking in masculinity and manliness. The literary portrayal is rooted in both formal and folk history. The folktale of John the slave and his master's women makes explicit use of this evocative ritual. John is pitted against a seven-foot-tall Black giant from a neighboring plantation. Despite the fact that John is smaller and lighter than his opponent, John's master stakes all of his wealth on the fighting prowess of his celebrated slave. John is no fool, and realizing that physically he is no match for his huge antagonist, he pits his wits against the bigger man's fists. On the day of the fight, both Blacks and whites gather to watch the much publicized contest. The Black giant struts around, showing off his magnificent physique and predicting that John will not even show up for the fight. John finally saunters onto the cleared field attired in evening dress, carrying a cane and white gloves, tipping his hat to friends in the crowd and occasionally adjusting the fit of his coat. He strolls over to where his master and mistress and their daughter are seated, says "afternoon" to his master, and slaps first the mistress then the daughter full in the face with his bare hand, tips his hat, turns and casually walks away. Everyone is astounded, but the Black giant, knowing that if John is bad enough to slap not one but two white women in full view of half the white men of the county, then killing a Black man will be like batting an eye, runs from the clearing, his pleas for mercy echoing behind him.

The point of the story is, of course, that the Black man who would be a man must come by way of the white woman. The encounter between Black man and white woman in the works under consideration here is something more than the obligatory coupling which has characterized interracial sexual relationships in much Black fiction. There is meaning in these encounters which goes beyond the sexual dimension of masculinity. The relationship is a necessary adjunct—but not always a catalyst—for the definition, or lack of definition, which the characters achieve as Black men.

Walker Vessels is the Slave. He attempts to posit for himself another version of masculinity, one rooted in his leadership of the bloody struggle to achieve political liberation for himself and his Black followers. At issue also, however, is his own struggle to make the political image of masculinity operative within his personal life. Grace, then, is not the citadel whose conquest symbolizes the attainment of power inherent in the concept of masculinity. Whatever the union with the white woman may have symbolized for Walker during their married life, it is obvious that Grace now represents for Walker his enslavement to the values of the Western world. His confrontation with Grace and her present husband does represent a victory of sorts for Walker, despite the fact that his personal and public images never quite jibe with each other. The definition which he seeks to internalize has been of his own, rather than the white woman's, posing. His failure to make the revolutionary image a part of his masculine self-concept is inherent in his need to kill his half-breed children, his still beloved wife, and his one-time friend. This failure is further objectified at the close of the play when Walker once again appears in the garb of the slave, the field hand, the ancient, yet ageless representative of caged Black manhood whose intelligence and potency are held captive by a mask of ragged senility.

Akin to Walker's positing of another referent for the symbol of the white woman is Marcus' transcendence of the limits inherent in the symbolic relationship between Black man and white woman. He regains in Louise's bed the feeling of control, of potency, lost in the fields under the goading of Louise's husband, which is necessary to his hard man self-image. Under the influence of Jim Kelly's quiet prodding and his developing awareness of Louise as a person, this streetman image is modified, expanded. The final test, then, is posed not in terms of Louise, but of Bonbon and the system of which he is the murderous instrument. Nor is the test to Marcus' masculinity. Rather, it is to his humanity. As with Walker, Marcus tests himself against his own self-imposed definitions. On one level, he seeks to define, to answer the question, Am I bad enough to fuck this white woman and die? On another, it is the question which must continually confront the streetman, Am

I as bad as I say I am, bold enough to do and bad enough to pay? But at its deepest level, the question posed by Marcus' actions is one of just how he chooses to see himself in relation to his history. In broadening, as he does, the arena in which he can be a man, he affects the course of his own personal history, coming at last into control of it, and he also, perhaps, affects the personal development of others on the Hebert Plantation.

Clay starts with the white woman—in accepting the apples which she offers, he also accepts the promise of her body—but he then moves to a place deep within himself where the white woman is irrelevant to his discovery of himself. In this he is similar to Marcus, but unlike Marcus, Clay tries to turn his back, to climb back within previously imposed limits. To some extent, this difference between Marcus' response and Clay's is predicated upon the relationships they have with the white woman. Louise's childish insipidness develops into a womanly self-consciousness while Lula's sterile sexuality remains unchanged by her contact with Clay. Lula is not programmed for human response. It makes little difference to her whether Clay continues with his bold assertions or retreats from his daring; she has sealed his fate from the moment he reveals his dangerous perceptiveness. More important is Marcus' intuitive understanding that self-knowledge, self-image, self-understanding, achieve reality only through action in the real world. Action objectifies the conscious and unconscious; manhood cannot remain a secret between a male and that which he has chosen to make an extension of himself—his clothes, his car, his horn or his penis. If one is Black, manhood must be defined out of one's self and against the definitions posited by the dominant society. Clay tries to by-side, evade, reality, failing to realize that reality will not by-side him.

Blues for Mister Charlie is unique in that, unlike the other works, the ritual of the Black man/white woman provides much of the dramatic tension in the play, yet Richard, under the loving influence of Juanita, quickly moves beyond his stylized responses to the symbolism embodied in the ritual. The scene in the Brittens' store where Richard tries to buy a coke and change a twenty-dollar bill is dominated by Richard's jibing mockery of the "citadel" which he is supposed to covet and admire. And it is as much Richard's derisive attitude toward the white woman, Jo, as it is his fight with the white man, Lyle, which precipitates Richard's death. For his actions reflect his feelings that the white woman is nothing more than a tired, "sad-assed chick" who satisfies no one and cannot herself be satisfied, a woman who is, in fact, irrelevant to anyone's definition of masculinity.

Blues is also unique in that Baldwin portrays a vitally alive Black woman as a contrast to the tired symbolism of the white woman. The potential for this sort of portrayal in *Of Love and Dust* lies, of course, in the characters of Pauline, Bonbon's Black concubine, and Louise, his child-like wife. But having sketched in the outlines of the contrast through juxtaposing Pauline's climb from field worker to house servant and Louise's impotent and inept rebellions against Bonbon, Gaines changes the terms in which the two characters must be viewed. The earthy vitality of Pauline, which Bonbon seeks in his liaison with her, is neutralized, for she has accepted the proscriptive limits set by the Big House on her relationship with Bonbon. Pauline, while well defined as a character, never really comes into her own as a person, always standing in the shadows of Bonbon or Louise, allowing their reality to define her own. Louise, however, develops a force and personality which must be reckoned with. Also in contrast to Pauline's passivity is Juanita's sinewy animation. Juanita is not merely Jo's opposite; she is several steps beyond the realm in which Jo plays out the joyless charade of married life in whitetown. She has a wise vitality, evident throughout the play, which culminates in her passionate speech on the witness stand in the third act of the play. She is the fecundity of the past, the Black American past, begun in the South, but also including, through the influence of Richard's life and death, that curious mixture of cynicism and hopefulness which is so characteristic of the continuing Black migrations to the Northern cities. Her continued fertility as Black mother and Black woman is symbolized in the children, hers and Richard's or hers and someone else's, who will be the living continuation of the long lines of Black people who have preceded her and Richard.

The protagonist dies, is murdered, in *Dutchman, Blues,* and *Of Love and Dust.* In *The Slave,* he is reduced to a death-in-life subsistence. These deaths are not coincidence, the outcome of a random convergence of ways in which to conclude literary works. On the contrary, Gaines, Baldwin and Baraka have on this point a common understanding, one which sees that Clay, Richard, Walker and Marcus, symbolic representational Black men, have been ripped off, done to death by the dominant society which sees no role for Black males except that of a grinning, dancing clown who is programmed to assume other dehumanized masks at the push of a button or a change in the tone of a white voice. And death is associated with the white woman because none but the most awe-filled reverential relationships with her are a part of the program.

There is variety in this presentation of their common point of view, for Clay and Walker live as they have died, in painful isolation. One must resort to rhetoric, the verbal slight of hand which holds that in creating a work of art a necessary and significant transcendence is gained over the situation which is portrayed in the work, in order to coerce a kind of triumph from the demise of Walker and Clay. While there is a certain validity in this attitude, it is cold comfort for those who would like triumph to take a more concrete form. But the end to estrangement and isolation which becomes such a significant aspect of the lives of Marcus and Richard is a concrete expression of the triumph which they achieve in life and which also transcends their dying. In dying, they leave others who have been influenced by and who understand the meaning of their life, the significance of their actions and their death. They are pictured as integral parts of a total cultural experience which does not cease as they cease. And this, the continuity of Black life, of that strong nigger feeling, is one of the chief themes in Neo-Black literature.

| III |

Amiri Baraka provided the first psalm and it is only appropriate that Don L. Lee sing the last. Baraka and Lee have, as vocal exponents of Neo-Black literature, come to symbolize most of what is strong and beautiful and vital in Black experience and Black art. And it is not straining the evocative power of metaphor to speak of them in terms of religious spirituality, for in Black life, the Music has as much power as the Word; these two poets are shamans of both. Thus the movement from Baraka to Lee is circular, not linear. Like these two in their works, this study has attempted to enclose, to encircle, to approach the center of an aspect of Blackness. Each poet speaks to the theme of the sustaining power of Black heritage in a different way. Baraka harks back to continuity and tradition, to those who carry "life from our ancestors," to the knowledge passed on to mother, passed on to *him* "and all the other Black people of our time." It is this heritage, this strong nigger feeling, which Juanita reawakens in Richard and which gives meaning and power to his life and death.

Lee's reference is almost specifically directed to the streetman-playboy preoccupied with his looks—and looking as white as hair slicked down with thick grease and plastered in place by a tight fitting cap made from the cut-off top of a stocking will allow—who is transformed into a silent walker with a careful eye who knows that in the coming world—the New World—the reality of being human and of responding to others as thinking, feeling people will take precedence over the acquisition of mere things as symbols of status. The same sense of tradition which dominates Baraka's poem enriches Lee's. The ironic and satiric eye with which Lee views the jo jo of the opening stanzas is softened when he speaks of jo jo's mother. The two views carry within them an implicit contrast, representing as they do, different aspects of a varied tradition. What would you do if someone loved you, Lee asks. His referent is not clear, but his very obscurity is indicative of the complexity of the patterns which bind mother to son, generation to generation, the slave to the freed man to the Neo-Black man.

This is the pattern which Gaines portrays so skillfully and so movingly, the pattern which binds Marcus to Kelly, to Aunt Ca'line and Aunt Margaret, even as he seeks to pull away and deny their hold, even as they attempt to quiet him and disown him. Neither the pattern nor the world of the pattern is new; but then, neither are any of the characters "instant negro." Through Marcus—who

approaches the transformation or conversion of jo jo—
James Kelly realizes that there is a "coming world/new
prizes are to be given," and because Kelly is a part of the
quarters, of Margaret and Ca'line and Charlie Jordan, his
knowledge must also be theirs. The force generated in
Marcus' rebellion does not end in his death, for his action
is its own conductor and its power is regenerated as it
passes through the quarters, shaking the foundation of all
the houses that slavery built.

The richness of relationships out of which come Richard and Marcus makes the sterility and paucity of the lives
of Clay and Walker all the more apparent. Clay and
Walker have been abstracted out of Black tradition, leaving as their only environment the brutal and oppressive
one of racism. They take no account, in their dealing with
the outside world, of the lessons of deception, manipulation and control taught by the streetman. Their only posture is one of frustrated rage and impotence which, even
when they try to act, suffocates them and reduces them to
slavery and death. They have not learned that the secret
to Black survival is Black love. And this is important, for
in *Blues for Mister Charlie* and *Of Love and Dust* the
streetman is not only a symbol of hardness, of that quality
which allows the best game runners in the Life to keep on
getting up in the face of success or defeat, but also a
symbol of an invigorating strength which renews the
streetman even as he helps to renew and revitalize Black
life. One sees these characters through a darkened glass

CONCLUSION

which reflects and refracts the vision. The Black world of
the Life slips away and one sees them in conflict with white
society, the society with which their life styles conflict, but
which they seldom touch.

In the realm of literature where Black writers are seeking to give concrete forms to Black experience in this
country, to posit and describe in all its varied facets the
large controlling images that give philosophic meaning to
the facts of ordinary life, to express the archetype which
in turn reveals hidden attitudes and experiences, the
Black writer is making not new gods, but a new language
and mythology. And perhaps by providing Black people
with another view of their experience, showing the basic
relationships between their own heroes and the rest of
society, these writers have provided another facet to the
prism of Black mythology. This is not the end:

> Here's the drum that is his head
> and the scale that is his logic
>
> Rolled on the streets of the niggers.

Call him down
Make him talk

And an explanation start.

Let the old men have it
Let the punks take it

And let the strong men who he loves use him and his ways
for the strength of the peoples
and the strength of the logic

GIVE BIRTH TO BRIGHTNESS

and his rest will be never, for the talk
he will inspire

Let him live, when he dies
and give birth to
brightness

Amiri Baraka
"Premises Not Quite Condemned"
Black Magic: Poetry 1961–1967

The Demands of Blackness on Contemporary Critics

In the late fifties or early sixties, the late rhythm and blues singer, Little Willie John, released his beautiful version of "The Masquerade Is Over." The song comes to mind now because I feel that throughout this work I have been engaging in an often trying but necessary masque of being the omniscient, objective critic. The part of the role which dictated that "one" be substituted for "I," "them" for "us," and "Black people" for "we," was trying. But necessity seemed to dictate my assumption of the critic's mask because I wanted to separate, as much as possible, my own personality from the ideas I have presented. One of the great pitfalls confronting Black writers—whether novelist, dramatist, essayist, poet or critic—is the tendency of others to deal with the self, the *I* presented, merely reading into the works rather than dealing with the works themselves. This is one of the most successful of the numerous ways of co-opting or neutralizing the Black artist. For if Baldwin is a punk, Ellison an Uncle Tom, Baraka a self-styled Messiah and Wright the victim of his own self-loathing, then the compelling ideas and issues raised in their works, which defy these ridiculous but convenient

231

categories, can be evaded or dismissed. A great deal of what passes for literary criticism of Black writers operates at just this level. And now that the One-Black-book-every-few-years rule has been broken, this assassination which invalidates a literary work through the destruction of the author's character may well become wholesale slaughter. So I confined myself to "one," "they," and "them." I think that the idea of a Black critic dealing with the works of Black writers within the framework of Black experience and Black literary history is important enough that it should not have to compete with any author's personality for attention.

Still, I do not feel Willie John's sadness now that my masquerade is over: can't take too much of a good thing. And "objective critics" have their limits. When objective critics begin to talk about any of the important issues which confront Black writers, they tend to sound very patronizing, very white. They run the risk of addressing themselves to an ill-defined and, I suspect, non-existent audience, of being called oreo or coconut or something worse. I do not play that stuff. None of the issues which I feel it necessary to discuss here is original with me. Black writers have been talking about these questions in conversations and in print for a number of years. But they bear repeating and rehashing because we have yet to confront them and deal with them successfully.

The first and least important issue is the whole controversy about the role of the white critic—and white writer—in Black literature. White critics and Black writers have been bound together in a necessary relationship because Black writers have always had to become "serious" artists by way of white critics. It is a rare Black writer who has not depended on good reviews from white critics to help him find an audience—almost always 99.9% white—for his books. (Only within the last five to ten years has the upsurge of interest in the Black past and the Black present, political upheaval and a modest prosperity enabled Black people to purchase books in significant numbers.) Now, white critics make and break "serious" white writers in much this same way. What has strained the relationship between Black writer and white critic is the presumption of white critics who attempt to dictate how Black writers should approach their material and even what that material should be, to psychoanalyze Black writers and Black readers and to generally reveal a gross ignorance under the ill-fitting guise of objectivity and critical authority. The strains in the relationship became most apparent with the publication of Ralph Ellison's rejoinder ("The World and the Jug," *New Leader*, Dec. 1963 and Feb. 1964) to Irving Howe's "Black Boys and Native Sons" and the relationship has never been the same since. The nadir was reached in 1967 when William Styron's *The Confessions of Nat Turner* was greeted with wild applause by white critics who knew nothing of the history or experience which Styron sought to portray. Through all the rumblings in between and since, one fact has emerged: White critics have only a miniscule place in Black literature. Sometimes, a white critics is perceptive enough to hit upon the outlines of Black literature, the universals which make literature, whether folk or formal, literature the world over. White critics have every right to comment upon any literature. But they have neither the right nor the authority to proclaim themselves "experts" on Black literature. Their validity as critics of Black literature has still to be established in the same way that we are establishing ours—through the acuteness of our insights and the clarity of our perceptions. With only the rarest exception, white critics have proved time and again that their perceptions are neither deep enough nor precise enough to give us the insights we need into our literature and our experience. As Black critics, we can make free use of the outlines and general perceptions which their writings may provide. But we must also remind them and the Black people to whom our work is addressed that their place in our literature is negligible.

Yet, even as we point out their errors and misconceptions, their sins of omission and commission, we must continue to develop our own ideas and themes. Poet Nikki Giovanni provides us with a beautiful analogy when she speaks of how white ignorance created, out of thin air, the so-called zombies of the vodun cults. The white man, not satisfied with that, has since reduced the zombie to a cocktail; we are no more important in his scale of values than a liquor to be sipped at his leisure. Won't it be a groove, she adds, when we have performed the same slight of hand on them, when we just walk into a bar and say, gimme a honkey, and have a glass of liquor appear in our hands. Perhaps we can't reach that point with white critics, at least not right away. But we can reduce them to their proper places, deal with them in glancing asides, in foot-notes, as the exotic and unimportant phenomena which any literary movement is bound to produce. And this is important, for Black literature requires our deepest at-tention. We waste time and energy devoting articles to refuting the ineptness of white critics, time and energy which is more profitably spent illuminating our literature.

In seeking to illuminate our literature, we must con-front a crucial question which is all too often by-sided in our attempts to prove how "revolutionary" or "relevant" or "serious" we are: What is our function as "Black" crit-ics? Is it an adjective which denotes our racial origins, or a quantifier signifying revolutionary zeal? If "Black" really has some definable and significant meaning when placed before "critics," then we must ask just how being "Black" modifies or alters the way in which we fill our roles as critics. Are we merely to set up aesthetic criteria or describe developing criteria within Black literature, are we developing the philosophical rationales upon which a viable literature can be based; or do we seek to translate Black literature into terms which the Black masses can understand? It seems to me that there is far more to the roles which Black critics must fill than these traditional functions of the critic. I'm not even sure of how valid these functions are, whether we can really translate all of them into Black terms. There is an inherent rhyme and rhythm to Black life; we know it because we feel it in our blood and hear it in our ears. I have only seen it defined in art, art as diverse as the sculpture of John Torres, the paintings of Charles Sebree, the novels of Barry Beckham and Nathan Heard or the poetry of Michael Harper. These men are coming from different places, and when they reach that point where history intersects their heartbeats, they make unique comments which resound against and illuminate our own views of that history, that experience. And if critics impose aesthetic standards which are general enough to give freedom to these few, don't we also run the risk of cutting off the necessary resonance from other writers who have just as much to tell us, to show us, to give us? I don't know. I do know that criticism must deal with the infinite number of ways in which the Black artist tries to capture, to imitate, to replay the intricate collage of Black life and experience. This is, of course, self-evident. It seems further that this collage of experience must be our critical touchstone.

It is not standards of aesthetics—beauty—which Black critics need to impose or even analyze. Nor can we settle the largely semantic question of what is Black, what is Negro, what colored. In literature, the distinction has meaning, for example, when it symbolizes the movement from one frame of reference to another, and the work

provides a given context by which we may judge the validity of the movement. The real world provides us with no
such concrete contexts. As one brother remarked of this
issue, we are all tainted in some way, to some degree, with
the white man. I also have to add that the power to make
these distinctions in the living Black experience resides
within our collective will, not in the whim of elitist groups
whose arbitrary definitions of these terms have further
divided the people they hope to unite. Black people are
like Black music, rich and varied, a people whose individ-
uality is formed, informed and re-formed out of common
experiences and group histories. There are many Black
experiences. To define one may be to exclude all others.
But to describe one is to speak about and to all the others.
In widening the scope for their conversations with Black
people, this is precisely what Black writers are doing.
We add another meaningful and necessary voice to this
conversation when we point out the subtle ways in which
one description relates to other experiences or relates to
the other areas of our life in America and how all have
meaning for the living. I swear that Baraka's poem,
"leroy," tells me the same thing as Richard's speech in
the third act of *Blues for Mr. Charlie* ("I feel like I'm beginning to understand my life—for the first time. I can
look back—and it doesn't hurt me like it used to"); both
touch the same theme as Lightnin' Hopkins' version of
"Going Down Slow," and it is no longer painful to see
ourselves in the memory of our mother's faces. The poem,

the play, the song and life converge and it is this point of convergence, which has its own inherent beauty, its own Blackness, which we must try to illuminate.

For as "arbitrators of taste"—or "BLACKNESS" we stand between Black people and Black writers and, inasmuch as our known ancestors were probably not glassmakers, we cloud rather than reveal or facilitate the exchange between artist and audience. Besides, Black people are perfectly capable of deciding what is "beautiful," what is Black and vital, in the literature which seeks to be ours in the same way that Black music is ours. And this shift of mine from Black critic to Black person is deliberate, for, like the artist, our common heritage and traditions bind us to Black people, even as the specialized skills which we bring to bear in analyzing that common heritage make us a smaller group within the larger one. The word, Black, before our quasi-professional title of "critic," however, is a means of affirming our sense of the common roots of all the individual members. And the word Black also symbolizes the implicit covenant we make with all other Black people that our work will be informed by a positive sense of that common past.

Our awareness of the covenant is communicated through the way in which we function as critics. As one part of that function we can show the relationships between varying aspects of experience. Our most important function, however, lies in examining the works of our writers to see how well they present their versions of Black life, even if those versions are not our own, to see what insights they are trying to reveal to us, to see if they have reworked the old stereotypes and themes and images to bring us more understanding of ourselves as individuals and as a group of fragmented, oppressed people. We are, then, not translators of meaning but interpreters who refract image and situation, plot and metaphor, character and symbol, illusion and theme through our knowledge of Black literature in its whole and its parts, through our study of the history and cultural expressions of Black people, through our personal experiences, in order to add another voice to the developing conversation between Black writers and Black people. And our collective voice will have its own distinct tone, its own unique information to impart.

Even as we add to or redefine just how we will function as Black critics, we must keep in mind the distinction between criticizing the works of an author and attacking the person of that author. The two are not the same. As contradictory as it may sound, together books are not necessarily written by together people—at least not the version of togetherness which may guide our own personal lives. But if a writer can get it together on the written page, that is all we as critics need concern ourselves with; we don't need to include the writer in our list of personal friends or most respected people. This gives us credibility as Black critics of Black literature, and perhaps Black writers will no longer assume that our negative comments about their works are statements of personal animosity. With Black experience as our critical touchstone, we can by-side the shaky ground which surrounds the narrowly defined concept of revolutionary fervor as a means of evaluating Black writing. Every piece of writing with choppy non-sentences, perverted word order and four letter words set in stanzaic form on a piece of paper and whose message consists of two different ways to say kill the honkey is not a poem, although its revolutionary zeal may be patent. And that's a fact, Jack. Perhaps if a manual on guerilla warfare were appended to these attempts at poetry, I could say more for their poetic content. This appendix would certainly evoke a new response to a message which had become moth-eaten long before it could attain meaning in the world of concrete objects. I'm not against repetition or even redundancy—perhaps if we chant "Black is beautiful" long enough, we will come to believe this, a process which must be the foundation for all other actions—but I am against those circular cries which put me to sleep or, worse, show me no way of breaking an unproductive, self-defeating cycle. Our revolution is not merely at the point of a gun. Rather, it is at the bottom of our hearts, at the back of our ideas of ourselves, in the forms which our relationships with each other take. It is these inner views of ourselves which Black writers are exploring and which we must now address ourselves to.

Despite our insistence that, because of our experiences as Blacks, we are, as critics of Black literature, more per-

ceptive about and responsive to the writings of other
Blacks, we seldom bring our Black experience to bear in
our critical writings. It is as though the only Black culture
we know exists within the covers of a book. We look at one
book to validate sociological and historical facts in another; we turn to militant writers to validate revolutionary
stances. But a vast area of interactions among Blacks is
left virtually untouched, as though Black literature not
only has no relevance for Blacks on an everyday level,
but does not touch or have significance for that life. One
either disagrees or agrees, for example, with the political
stance of Amiri Baraka; but he is saying so much more to
Black people than "kill the honkey"—which after all
takes little literary talent—or even love Black. His works
are an anthology of Black experiences, Black interactions,
Black perceptions and insights. To reduce them to the
level of political rhetoric or nationalist jargon does him
a great disservice and robs Black people of one of their
greatest natural resources: the fuller significance of the
work of our artists. What is true of Baraka is true of Baldwin, of Harper and other lesser known writers.

Instead of using our experiences as Blacks as a means
of tapping that area of interaction which is generally
closed to non-Blacks, we evoke our Black lives through re-
course to dues paying, the price we must pay in order to
get through the world. Now the world extracts some pay-
ment from everyone for allowing them to exist. The sur-
charge which this society extracts from Black people is
onerous; we pay it in personal and private humiliations,

in public subjugation. I think it was Baldwin who made the term dues-paying widely known, but since his time it has come to mean a specialized form of pain and privation which only the very poor, the convict, the drug addict, perhaps the survivors of those first voter registration drives in the South have known. This kind of experience becomes the primary criterion by which one is qualified to discuss or analyze aspects of Black life. The criterion is so rigidly drawn that at least one poet of middle-class background finds it necessary to speak of that background as though it were lived in the meanest poverty—in order to give the poetry an "authentic" ring. As a means of validating literary critics and others who would speak about Black experience with authority, dues-paying is a rather poor measure. It is more to the point, for example, to allow this book to stand on its own merits rather than discussing the nature or depth of my own dues-paying— which after all concerns no one but myself and my family —in order to "verify" my credentials or to titillate an audience.

Give Birth to Brightness is an attempt to respond to the issues which I have raised in this Afterword. But there are other critics whose writings are an example of the kind of meaningful criticism which is as necessary to the continued vitality of Black literature as the dynamite writers who are being published in increasingly larger numbers. Hoyt Fuller, the editor of *Black World*, consistently provides excellent criticism in the reviews he occasionally writes for the magazine. That he is working within a Neo-Black, even a revolutionary, framework, is obvious, and his insights and perceptions, his ability to articulate, to communicate his understanding of Black literature and Black experience and the diverse relationships between the two is seldom equaled by any other critic that I know of. I have heard novelist Paule Marshall deliver a lecture characterized by precise insights and a deep understanding of the relationship between revolutionary consciousness and Black writing. Yet, this is precisely the kind of criticism which is generally overlooked in favor of flashy personality slashing, pseudo-revolutionary fervor and the cryptic mysticism which confuses rather than clarifies. Marshall and Fuller are daring in their criticism and in daring to be wrong they help to generate the kinds of discussions which create viable philosophical tenets for Black criticism. There must be no end to these discussions.

Bibliography

This is a selected bibliography of works which have not been previously cited in the body of the text. The works which have the most direct bearing upon this study have already been noted; they are repeated here only where I felt it necessary to give additional and pertinent bibliographical information usually other dates and places of publication. The most comprehensive source on Black writers and Black writing from 1853 to 1969 is Darwin Turner's *Afro-American Literature* (New York, 1970). *Phylon: Review of Race and Culture*, from Atlanta University, publishes an annual review of literature by and about Blacks. *Black World* (formerly *Negro Digest*) is an open forum for writers from many different genres and political persuasions. The monthly book reviews are often written by the best of the younger writers and contain valuable perceptions about the works reviewed as well as analyses of how the works relate to the current literary scene. The *Journal of Black Poetry* (published in San Francisco) and *Black Theatre* (published in New York) are also important literary forums.

Rather than duplicating the general sources readily available in Turner and *Phylon*, I have listed pertinent bibliographical information for Baldwin, Baraka and Gaines. The sources which follow this section are, with the exception of the anthologies, non-critical. The anthologies are listed because in many cases they contain literary selections which are not readily available elsewhere, and because often the introductions to otherwise well-known selections are excellent pieces of criticism. The non-critical sources are, for me, almost as important as the works of the authors who have been the subjects of this discussion. They provide the necessary historical, cultural and literary background for analyzing and understanding the literature as an aspect of Black cultural expression.

Except in rare instances, the material cited here is available in inexpensive reprints or paperback editions.

244

BIBLIOGRAPHY

| I |

JAMES BALDWIN

Baldwin, James. *The Amen Corner.* New York, 1968.
———. *Another Country.* New York, 1962.
———. *Blues for Mister Charlie.* New York, 1964.
———. *The Fire Next Time.* New York, 1963.
———. *Giovanni's Room.* New York, 1956.
———. *Go Tell It on the Mountain.* New York, 1963.
———. *Going to Meet the Man.* New York, 1965.
———. *Nobody Knows My Name.* New York, 1961.
———. *Notes of a Native Son.* Boston, 1955.
———. *Tell Me How Long the Train's Been Gone.* New York.
  1968.

Criticism

Alexander, Charlotte A. *Baldwin's "Go Tell It on the Mountain"*
  . . . *and Other Works.* New York, 1966.
Eckman, Fern. *The Furious Passage of James Baldwin.* New
  York, 1966.
Featherstone, Joseph. "Blues for Mr. Baldwin," *New Republic,*
  Vol. 153 (Nov. 27, 1965), 34–36.
Finn, James. "James Baldwin's Vision," *Commonweal,* Vol. 78
  (July 26, 1963), 447–449.
———. "The Identity of James Baldwin," *Commonweal,* Vol. 77
  (Oct. 26, 1962), 113–116.
Gibson, Donald B., ed. *Five Black Writers.* New York, 1970.
Hagopian, John V. "James Baldwin: The Black and the Red,
  White and Blue," *CLA Journal,* VII (1964), 133–140.
Hernton, Calvin C. "Blood of the Lamb," *Amistad,* I, i, (1970).
Isaacs, Harold R. "Five Writers and Their African Ancestors:
  Part II," *Phylon,* XXI, iii (1960), 317–336.
Kent, George E. "Baldwin and the Problem of Being," *CLA
  Journal,* VII (1964), 202–214.

Lash, John S. "Baldwin Beside Himself: A Study in Modern Phallicism," *CLA Journal,* VIII (1964), 132–140.
MacInnes, Colin. "Dark Angel: The Writings of James Baldwin," *Encounter,* XX (1963).

AMIRI BARAKA (LEROI JONES)

Baraka, Imamu Amiri (LeRoi Jones) and Fundi (Billy Abernathy [photographer]). *In Our Terribleness (Some Elements and Meaning in Black Styles).* Indianapolis & New York, 1969.
Jones, LeRoi. *The Baptism and The Toilet.* New York, 1967.
———. *Black Arts.* Newark, N.J., 1966.
———. *Black Magic: Poetry 1961–1967.* Indianapolis & New York, 1969.
———. *Black Music.* New York, 1968.
———. *Blues People.* New York, 1963.
———. *The Dead Lecturer.* New York, 1964.
———. *Dutchman and The Slave.* New York, 1964.
———. *Four Black Revolutionary Plays.* Indianapolis & New York, 1969.
———. *Home: Social Essays.* New York, 1966.
———. *Jello.* Chicago, 1970.
———. *Preface to a Twenty-Volume Suicide Note.* New York, 1961.
———. *The System of Dante's Hell.* New York, 1965.
———. *Tales.* New York, 1967.
Jones, LeRoi, ed. *The Moderns: An Anthology of New Writings in America.* New York, 1963.
Jones, LeRoi and Larry Neal, eds. *Black Fire.* New York, 1968.

Criticism

Cook, Mercer and Stephen E. Henderson. *The Militant Black Writer in Africa and the United States.* Madison & London, 1969.

BIBLIOGRAPHY

Costello, Donald P. "Black Man as Victim," *Commonweal*, Vol. 88 (June 28, 1968), 436–440.

Jackson, Kathryn. "LeRoi Jones and the New Black Writers of the Sixties," *Freedomways*, IX, iii (1969), 232–247.

Neal, Larry. "The Black Arts Movement," *The Drama Review* XII iv T40 (1968), 32–37.

Riley, Clayton, ed. *A Black Quartet*. New York, 1970.

———. "On Black Theater," Addison Gayle, Jr. *The Black Aesthetic*. Garden City, N.Y., 1971, 313–330.

ERNEST GAINES

Gaines, Ernest. *The Autobiography of Miss Jane Pittman*. New York, 1971.

———. *Bloodline*. New York, 1968.

———. *Catherine Carmier*. New York, 1964.

———. *Of Love and Dust*. New York, 1967.

Criticism

Bryant, Jerry. "Politics and the Black Novel," *The Nation*, Vol. 212 (April 5, 1971), 436–438.

| II |

Fiction and Drama

Beckham, Barry. *My Main Mother*. New York, 1969.

Bontemps, Arna. *Drums at Dusk*. New York, 1939.

Bullins, Ed. *Five Plays*. Indianapolis & New York, 1969.

Chesnutt, Charles. *The House Behind the Cedars*. New York, 1900; Toronto, 1968.

Cullen, Countee. *One Way to Heaven*. New York, 1932.

DuBois, W.E.B. *Dark Princess*. New York, 1928.

———. *The Quest of the Silver Fleece*. London, 1911; Miami, Fla., 1969.

Dunbar, Paul Lawrence. *The Strength of Gideon and Other Stories*. New York, 1969.

Elder, Lonnie. *Ceremonies in Dark Old Men*. New York, 1969.

Griggs, Sutton. *Imperium In Imperio*. 1899; New York, 1969.

Heard, Nathan. *Howard Street*. New York, 1968.

Kelley, William Melvin. *A Different Drummer*. New York, 1962.

———. *A Drop of Patience*. New York, 1965.

Killens, John O. *And Then We Heard the Thunder*. New York, 1963.

Mahoney, William. *Black Jacob*. Toronto & London, 1969.

Major, Clarence. *All Night Visitors*. New York, 1969.

Mayfield, Julian. *The Hit*. New York, 1957.

Ottley, Roi. *White Marble Lady*. New York, 1965.

Petry, Ann. *The Street*. New York, 1946.

Pharr, Robert Dean. *The Book of Numbers*. Garden City, N.Y., 1969.

Philips, Jane. *Mojo Hand*. New York, 1966.

Schuyler, George. *Black No More*. New York, 1931 & 1969.

Toomer, Jean. *Cane*. New York, 1923 & 1966.

Van Vechten, Carl. *Nigger Heaven*. New York, 1926.

Webb, Frank J. *The Garies and Their Friends*. London, 1857; New York, 1969.

Williams, John A. *Night Song*. New York, 1961.

———. *Sons of Darkness, Sons of Light*. New York, 1969.

Wright, Richard. *Uncle Tom's Children*. New York, 1940 & 1965.

———. *Native Son*. New York, 1940 & 1966.

Poetry

Clifton, Lucille. *Good Times*. New York, 1969.

Evans, Mari. *I Am a Black Woman*. New York, 1970.

Giovanni, Nikki. *Black Judgement*. Detroit, 1968.

Harper, Michael. *Dear John, Dear Coltrane*. Pittsburgh, Pa., 1970.

BIBLIOGRAPHY

————. *History Is Your Own Heartbeat*. Urbana, Illinois, 1971.
Knight, Etheridge. *Poems from Prison*. Detroit, 1968.
Lee, Don L. *Black Pride*. Detroit, 1968.
————. *We Walk the Way of the New World*. Detroit, 1970.
Wright, Jay. *Death As History*. New York, 1967.
X, Marvin, *Fly to Allah*. Fresno, Calif., 1969.
Young, Al. *Dancing*. New York, 1964.

Anthologies

Alhamisi, Ahmed and Hauem Kofi Wangara, eds. *Black Arts*. Detroit, 1969.
Baker, Huston A., ed. *Black Literature in America*. New York, 1970.
Brown, Sterling, Arthur P. Davis, *et al. The Negro Caravan*. New York, 1941.
Chametzky, Jules and Sidney Kapland, eds. *Black and White in American Culture*. Amherst, Mass., 1969.
Chapman, Abraham, ed. *Black Voices*. New York, 1968.
Franklin, John Hope, ed. *Three Negro Classics* [Booker T. Washington, *Up from Slavery*, 1901; W.E.B. DuBois, *The Souls of Black Folk*, 1903; James Weldon Johnson, *Autobiography of An Ex-Colored Man*, 1912]. New York, 1965.
Hill, Herbert, ed. *Anger and Beyond: The Negro Writer in the United States*. New York, 1966.
————, ed. *Soon One Morning*. New York, 1963.
Jones, LeRoi and Larry Neal, eds. *Black Fire*. New York, 1968.
Jordon, June, ed. *Soulscript*. New York, 1970.
Knight, Etheridge, ed. *Black Voices from Prison*. New York, 1970.
Leslau, Charlotte and Wolf, eds. *African Proverbs*. New York, 1962.
Major, Clarence, ed. *The New Black Poetry*. New York, 1969.
Randall, Dudley, ed. *Black Poetry*. Detroit, 1969.

Randall, Dudley and Margaret G. Burroughs, eds. *For Malcolm.* Detroit, 1969.

Schulberg, Budd. *From the Ashes: Voices of Watts.* New York, 1967.

Williams, John A., ed. *Beyond the Angry Black.* New York, 1966.

Autobiography

Brown, Claude, *Manchild in the Promised Land.* New York, 1965.

Curtin, Philip D., ed. *Africa Remembered. Narratives by West Africans from the Era of the Slave Trade.* Madison & London, 1967.

Douglass, Frederick. *Life and Times of* .... 1892; London, 1962.

————. *My Bondage and My Freedom.* 1855; New York, 1969.

————. *Narrative of the Life of Frederick Douglass.* 1845; New York, 1968.

Holiday, Billie, with William Duffy. *Lady Sings the Blues.* New York, 1956 & 1969.

Hughes, Langston. *The Big Sea.* New York, 1940 & 1963.

————. *I Wonder As I Wander.* New York, 1956 & 1964.

Jackson, George. *Soledad Brother.* New York, 1970.

Johnson, James Weldon. *Along This Way.* New York, 1933 & 1968.

McKay, Claude. *A Long Way from Home.* New York, 1937 & 1970.

Thomas, Piri. *Down These Mean Streets.* New York, 1967.

Ward, Samuel Ringold. *Autobiography of a Fugitive Negro.* London, 1855; Chicago, 1970.

Wright, Richard, *Black Boy.* New York, 1945 & 1966.

History, Social and Psychological Interpretations

Chace, William M. and Peter Collier. *Justice Denied.* New York, 1971.

BIBLIOGRAPHY

Coles, Robert. *Children of Crisis: A Study in Courage and Fear.* Boston, 1967.

Franklin, John Hope. *From Slavery to Freedom.* New York, 1947, 1956, 1967.

Frazier, Franklin, *Black Bourgeoisie.* New York & London, 1957, 1965.

Herskovits, Melville. *The Myth of the Negro Past.* New York, 1941; Boston, 1958.

Hughes, Douglas A., ed. *From A Black Perspective.* New York, 1970.

Meltzer, Milton, ed. *In Their Own Words: A History of the American Negro.* New York, 1965.

Poussaint, Alvin F. "A Negro Psychiatrist Explains the Negro Psyche," *The New York Times Magazine,* Aug. 20, 1967.

Still, William. *The Underground Railroad.* 1871; Chicago, 1970.

Walker, David. *David Walker's Appeal.* Introduction by Charles M. Wiltse. New York, 1829 & 1965.

Music and Folklore

Addo, Peter, ed. *Ghana Folk Tales.* New York, 1968.

Berendt, Joachim. *The New Jazz Book.* New York, 1959.

Brewer, J. Mason. *American Negro Folklore.* Chicago, 1968.

Butcher, Margaret Just. *The Negro in American Culture.* New York, 1956.

Charters, Samuel. *The Poetry of the Blues.* New York, 1963.

Dorson, Richard M. *American Negro Folktales.* Bloomington, Ind., 1958.

Hentoff, Nat. *The Jazz Life.* New York, 1961.

Hodeir, Andre. *Jazz: Its Evolution and Its Essence.* New York, 1956.

Hughes, Langston and Arna Bontemps. *The Book of Negro Folklore.* New York, 1958.

Jackson, Bruce. *The Negro and His Folklore.* Austin, Tex. & London, 1967.

Jahn, Janheinz. *Muntu*. New York, 1961.

Keil, Charles. *Urban Blues*. Chicago, 1966.

Locke, Alain. *The Negro and His Music and Negro Art Past and Present*. 1936; New York, 1969.

Shaw, Arnold. *The World of Soul*. New York, 1970.

Spellman, A.B. *Four Lives in the BeBop Business*. New York, 1966.

Szwed, Joan F., ed. *Black America*. New York & London, 1970.

Williams, Martin T. *The Art of Jazz*. New York, 1959.